For Lucy, Ben, Isaac, and Freddy
for their inspiration and love

For the grandparent army whose love
and time helped me write this book

For all the students, teachers, parents,
and principals who taught me
how to do school social work

THE DOMAINS AND DEMANDS OF SCHOOL SOCIAL WORK PRACTICE

OXFORD WORKSHOP SERIES:

SCHOOL SOCIAL WORK ASSOCIATION OF AMERICA

Series Advisory Board

Evidence-Based Practice in School Mental Health
James C. Raines

The Domains and Demands of School Social Work Practice
Michael S. Kelly

Solution-Focused Brief Therapy in Schools
Michael S. Kelly, Johnny S. Kim, and Cynthia Franklin

THE DOMAINS AND DEMANDS
OF SCHOOL SOCIAL WORK PRACTICE

A Guide to Working Effectively With Students, Families, and Schools

Michael S. Kelly

OXFORD WORKSHOP SERIES

OXFORD
UNIVERSITY PRESS

2008

OXFORD
UNIVERSITY PRESS

Oxford University Press, Inc., publishes works that further
Oxford University's objective of excellence
in research, scholarship, and education.

Oxford New York
Auckland Cape Town Dar es Salaam Hong Kong Karachi
Kuala Lumpur Madrid Melbourne Mexico City Nairobi
New Delhi Shanghai Taipei Toronto

With offices in
Argentina Austria Brazil Chile Czech Republic France Greece
Guatemala Hungary Italy Japan Poland Portugal Singapore
South Korea Switzerland Thailand Turkey Ukraine Vietnam

Copyright © 2008 by Oxford University Press, Inc.

Published by Oxford University Press, Inc.
198 Madison Avenue, New York, New York 10016

www.oup.com

Library of Congress Cataloging-in-Publication Data
Kelly, Michael S. (Michael Stokely), 1968–
The domains and demands of school social work practice: a guide to
working effectively with students, families, and schools/Michael S.Kelly.
p. cm.—(Oxford workshop series : School Social Work
Association of America)
Includes bibliographical references and index.
ISBN 978-0-19-534330-4
1. School social work—United States. 2. Evidence-based
social work—United States. I. Title.
LB3013.4.K44 2008
371.4'6—dc22   2007052838

1 3 5 7 9 8 6 4 2

Printed in the United States of America
on acid-free paper

Contents

Contents

Preface: Trying Things

I remember the day I was first hired as a school social worker: May 17, 1993. It's not hard, as it was also the same day I was interviewed for the job. That morning, I had sat around a table with my school district's HR person, my eventual school principal, and the director of special education. The interview had gone well, and that afternoon they offered me the job. I have this mind's eye memory of running down the street in excitement, eager to get home and tell my fiancée and parents. That night Michael Jordan hit the game-winning shot to put away the Cleveland Cavaliers in the NBA playoff semifinals.

Since I was about to finish college, I knew that I wanted to be a school social worker, and now after 2 years of full-time master's course work, including a yearlong internship in a high school, here I was, the school social worker at a large junior high school in Chicago's suburbs.

Then a slow, creeping feeling of dread began to make its way into me. It began to dawn on me that I was alone in this new position, and that unlike many of my other friends in social work who had taken jobs in agencies or large nonprofits, I was going to be the only social worker in a building of 50 faculty and 1200 students. I was new, excited, passionate, and terrified.

My wise school social work supervisor had encouraged me to "go with the panic" and schedule a meeting with my new principal to see what ideas she had for my first year on the job. It was summer, so getting meetings with her wasn't hard, and she agreed to meet with me a few days later. I walked in and she immediately told me how excited she was to have me because the "last few school social workers we had weren't so great." She told me she was a former school counselor and that improving and protecting the mental health of students was a high priority for her. I asked her to give me a sense of what she wanted me to do this year, and her response was what I was to learn was typical of her: short and cryptic. "I want you to try things. The last two school social workers we had just sat there. Get out there and try things."

This book may not find you in the place I've just described, but I imagine that you too have a story about your first school job. Was your first job as a school social worker like it was for me, and did you have all that attendant first-job wooziness and anxiety? Or maybe you were moving into schools after practicing in other social work settings, and thought of it as just another way to share your skills with students, parents, and teachers. Whatever your initial state of mind, you likely reached a point early on in your school social work practice where you realized that the job you had signed up for had changed, or maybe even deepened. You had joined this complicated, confusing, thrilling social organization known as a school, and beyond whatever was in your job description (assuming, of course, you had one; I never had one in 14 years of practice in two school districts), you knew that there were areas you wanted to practice in, people you wanted to help, but...how?

This book represents my attempt to marshal the most current and rigorous evidence on key aspects of school social work practice to help school social workers address the multiple Yoles they are expected to fulfill and be effective in doing so. The problems and case examples in this book will hopefully remind you of your own challenging cases. The difference is that with some of the skills, resources, and perspectives offered in this book, you might be able to look at your challenging cases anew and come back to your work recharged and ready to, as my first principal said, "Get out and try things."

THE DOMAINS AND DEMANDS OF SCHOOL SOCIAL WORK PRACTICE

I

■ ■ ■

Introduction: School Social Work in the 21st Century—Making Evidence-Based Practice (EBP) Work in School Social Work Practice

School Social Work Is in Its Second Century: How Are We Doing?

School social work is one of social work's oldest subspecialties and just entered its second century. In the United States, school social work has grown from a few "visiting teachers" in 1906 working in community schools in Boston, New York, Hartford, and Chicago to a profession that now numbers over 20,000, having a national and more than 30 state associations (School Social Work Association of America [SSWAA], 2005). Internationally, recent estimates place school social work in over 40 countries, with over 50,000 practitioners (Huxtable, 2006).

School social work is alive and (relatively) doing well, and in some areas, like in Illinois, where I have practiced and taught for the past 15 years, appears to be growing. But what's behind these numbers of school social workers? What are school social workers actually doing in their positions? And in the spirit of this volume, what kinds of interventions are they using, and what does the best available evidence tell us about what school social workers might do to make their practices even more effective?

Individual Treatment in Schools: Are We Clinicians, Something Close, or Not Quite?

One of the persistent issues I hear when I give presentations about school social work is the notion that school social work needs to decide if it is a clinical social work job or not. Some states (like Illinois) have seemed to embrace the clinical role wholeheartedly, and many colleagues I've worked with over the years have described their work as a version of doing psychotherapy in a school setting. Other colleagues I've met from other states (California and Indiana come to mind) eschew the "clinician" tag and instead portray their work as more akin to a school-based consultant, working with teachers, students, parents, and administrators to create and implement behavior plans for students. Still others have characterized their school social work practice in terms of their acting as a prevention specialist, designing programs to increase social-emotional learning (SEL) for all students and addressing topical issues such as bullying or school violence (Anderson-Butcher, Iachini, & Wade-Mdivanian, 2007; Staudt, Cherry, & Watson, 2005).

The national associations (SSWAA and National Association of Social Workers [NASW]), in their mission statements, tend to sidestep the clinical/macro-practice distinction, emphasizing the "unique knowledge and skills" school social workers bring to multiple school contexts (SSWAA, 2005) and the range of individual, group, community organizing, and policy development skills necessary to practice as a school social worker (NASW, 2002). Though a range of practice modalities may be discussed by national school social work leaders and researchers, the tendency to view school social work through a clinical lens appears to be growing in the professional literature that documents actual practice (Allen-Meares, 1994; Johnson-Reid, Kontak, Citerman, Essma, & Fezzi, 2005; Staudt et al., 2005).

Some of these questions about school social work practice are almost as old as the profession itself. As Shaffer (2007) and Allen-Meares (1993) have noted, the field of school social work has struggled for years to adequately define its professional identity and capture the complexity of the many different roles school social workers play in their schools. This book won't settle that struggle because school social work is still too broadly defined across a variety of practice settings for there to be one national definition that has any validity. However, this is not true of all school-based mental health professions. School psychologists appear to have fairly uniform training requirements and practice roles across the 50 states, while school counselors have similar variability in school social work professional requirements (Altshuler, 2006).

It is certainly challenging to generalize about school social work roles and practices in the United States, but some important framing questions can at least get things started in thinking about the different ways by which school social workers might learn how to make their practice (whatever it is) more rooted in EBP. The following questions will help organize this book and provide clues to what is known about school social work practice in 2008:

- Are school social workers still working with mostly students with individualized treatment plans, and are they doing so within traditional clinical service delivery models?
- Are they employing EBP interventions to help students, or are they relying on "practice as usual" interventions that may or may not be effective?
- More to the point, what do they consider are their preferred "practice as usual" interventions and what can be done to highlight effective practices in these areas?
- To what degree are school social workers serving their whole school population through more systemic and prevention-oriented practice, designed to help students, parents, and teachers and improve the overall learning environment of their particular school?

All School Social Work Is Local

To understand the nature of practice in schools better, the first concept that will be defined and discussed is school social work practice. A historical perspective, as well as current demographic data and labor statistics, will be delineated from local, national, and international perspectives. The second concept addressed in this book is EBP, which will be defined as a process by which school social workers can access the best current evidence to address client problems in a collaborative and culturally competent fashion (Gibbs, 2003). But ultimately, this book will be most effective to the degree that it allows school social workers to apply and implement these ideas in their own school and their own local context. To paraphrase Tip O'Neill (1995), all school social work is local, and the challenge for school social workers is to adapt the process of EBP to their own school and make it work for them, and most important, for their school clients.

School Social Work Challenges in 2007: No Child Left Behind (NCLB), Response to Intervention (RTI), Outcomes-Based Practice, and Specialization

This book will also denote the numerous challenges to school social work practice that are *not* local and are in fact coming from state and federal laws and policies, as well as general trends in this field. I believe that the EBP process outlined in this book will help school social workers both understand and cope with these issues in their day-to-day practice. There are at least four major challenges that this book will help school social workers navigate:

NCLB: The 2002 federal legislation was arguably the farthest-reaching piece of federal education legislation since the special educations laws of Individuals with Disabilities Education Improvement Act (IDEA) in the 1970s (Anderson, 2005). As most educators know by now, it established numerous benchmarks for student performance and created accountability mechanisms for schools that were not meeting adequate yearly progress (AYP) targets (U.S. Department of Education, 2005). What is often less understood is how much NCLB has focused attention on educators (including school social workers) becoming "highly qualified" to do their jobs in schools (Constable & Alvarez, 2006), with the concept being that all educators needed additional training to demonstrate their competence and proficiency. Additionally, NCLB requires educators to use "scientific, research-based" interventions over 100 times (NCLB, 2002; Raines, 2007), clearly making the kind of EBP process skills you will learn in this book a priority for school social workers wanting to survive and thrive under NCLB. Though it is likely that the reauthorization debate in Congress for NCLB in 2008 will modify some of the more controversial aspects of the legislation, the notion that schools and educators should be focused on using research-based interventions to meet measurable goals is unlikely to change. This is in part due to the multiple sources that are advocating for EBP in schools (i.e., special education laws, response to intervention, parent advocates), and these sources have only grown more interested in using data and evidence to improve student outcomes in the years since NCLB was passed by Congress.

RTI: In the midst of the upheavals wrought by NCLB, the special education law IDEA was reauthorized in 2004 and a new provision was added to allow districts to implement their own RTI program (IDEA, 2004). RTI is intended to be an early-intervention approach to help remove barriers to learning for students before they are referred for traditional special education assessment and services (Fuchs & Fuchs, 2001). While different RTI programs differ on the basis of individual school district needs (there's that dictum that all practice is ultimately local again!), it is clear that the RTI movement has some key general principles that focus on targeting early academic, counseling, and behavioral supports to students based on data-driven instruction, local assessments, and EBPs (Fuchs & Fuchs, 2001). Again, an EBP process like the one described in this book will be crucial to helping school social workers contribute fully to RTI initiatives underway in their school community.

Outcomes-Based Education: Related to NCLB, but a movement all on its own, outcomes-based education challenges school social workers to demonstrate that their interventions actually make a measurable difference in student achievement. The need for school social workers to document their practice with students is nothing new. Almost every school social worker I know has to write treatment plans, prepare Individualized Education Program (IEP) goals, and do other paperwork that describes the goals they have for their work with students. What's changed is that rather than making paperwork primarily an issue of compliance (completing paperwork and making sure it's stored properly), paperwork is now needed to demonstrate that school social workers can deliver the outcomes that schools, parents, and students are demanding (Newsome, 2004; Sipple & Banach, 2006). This book's EBP process will enable school social workers to write goals and implement interventions that are rooted in empirical findings and will also give practitioners more insights into how they might find valid and reliable measures of practice to demonstrate their client's progress.

Specialization: School social work is not yet a fully specialized subspecialty of social work in all states. Only 31 U.S. states have a state certification process for school social workers working in a school, and many states don't require master's-level training for school social workers to work in a school (Altshuler, 2006). The international school social work field, although growing, has few countries that have settled on criteria for certifying school social workers (of the 40 countries that have school social work, only Finland and China require a Master of Social Work [MSW] to practice in a school) (Huxtable, 2006). Despite the diversity in school social work certification, it is clear that the national trend will be to move school social workers to more specialized training and degrees, particularly given the mandates of NCLB

(Altshuler, 2006; Constable & Alvarez, 2006). Indiana has already implemented a statewide post-master's certification program that requires school social workers from Indiana to show through a portfolio assessment that they can implement EBPs in their work (Constable & Alvarez, 2006). Designing advanced training programs that enable school social workers to stay current with the best available evidence is a goal of the Loyola University Chicago's Family and Schools Partnership Program (FSPP). I will share the basic curriculum of the program as another example of how to bring an EBP process to future specialization efforts statewide, nationally, and internationally.

SEL, Barriers to Learning: New Opportunities for School Social Work to Show Its Stuff

Since the early 1990s, school researchers have been exploring ways to measure students' levels of "emotional intelligence" (Goleman, 1997; Seligman, 1995). This interest in emotional intelligence led to the study of SEL, and a burgeoning literature in this field has followed, led by researchers at the Collaborative for Academic, Social, and Emotional Learning (CASEL), based at the University of Illinois at Chicago. The CASEL researchers define SEL as a process by which all people in a school (children and adults) develop "fundamental emotional and social competencies" to help them learn how to name emotional states, develop empathy for others, and solve problems in challenging situations (CASEL, 2007, p. 1). Which school social worker doesn't want to help students develop these capacities?

It gets better—SEL may prove to be essential for decreasing discipline problems and increasing test scores. A recent meta-analysis of SEL programs has shown that programs and school-wide SEL programs can help students improve their behavior, self-concepts, and overall school achievement (Weissberg & Durlak, 2007).

A central problem for any school hoping to implement more SEL programming is ultimately less about the best program than about the people implementing the program. In many schools, the question nags: Who's going to create the programs, garner school and community support, run the programs, and evaluate their impacts? Researchers who have taken a look at implementation of SEL programs have found that key SEL leaders who know the school well and can access resources are essential to implementing the program and maintaining its success (Greenberg et al., 2003). With the emphasis school social workers place on helping a child using the person-in-environment framework (Raines, 2007), as well as our role of often serving the students with the most SEL-related needs, it would seem that school social workers could be well suited to becoming SEL leaders in their school communities. However, it is unclear whether this is in fact occurring because other related disciplines like school psychology, school counseling, public health, and school nursing make their bids to become known for their role in prevention and SEL programming. Through the chapters that follow, a number of interventions and strategies rooted in SEL research, as well as examples of how school social workers nationwide have stepped into SEL leadership roles in their schools, will be highlighted.

Doing the EBP Process With a Superintendent: The Case of the School Intruder

One morning in the fall of 2004, a young man angrily left his girlfriend's house in town and drove wildly down our main street. Police reports later revealed that the man was high on cocaine and had come to his girlfriend's house demanding that she give him money. When she refused, he drove away and crashed his car a block away from our school. He ran into our building, entering the only door that was open for a parent-teacher conference. The teacher and parents sitting there were startled but unharmed. The man went straight to the school office. The principal Mr. Calloway (not his real name) saw the intruder, who was walking fast through the hall visibly agitated. Not knowing whether the intruder was a parent or not, the principal escorted him to the office, found out from a teacher that the man was in fact an intruder, and quickly called 911. The man started making threats to the school secretary Mrs. Jones ("Get me out of here or I'll get you!"). Luckily, the police arrived quickly and the man was led out of the front of our school in handcuffs.

None of the students had seen him come or go because the man had entered our building when they were not at school. The only adults who were directly involved with him were the principal Mr. Calloway, the school secretary Mrs. Jones, and the kindergarten teacher and the two parents who were with her. Although few people knew about the incident, our school superintendent immediately arrived at our school, as I was sitting talking about the incident with Mr. Calloway. The superintendent told me and Mr. Calloway that he thought we needed to implement our school's crisis plan, which involved the use of Critical Stress Incident Debriefing (CSID) with the whole faculty and, if needed, students as well.

I knew intuitively that CSID was a bad idea for this situation, and said so to my principal and the superintendent. Few people had witnessed the incident, and they might be actually made more upset by having it recounted by people who went through it first-hand. Additionally, the incident was a seemingly random occurrence and might have no long-lasting effects on the school provided we shared accurate information with teachers, parents, and students. Why not, I suggested, just privately debrief with the persons involved and offer them support and possible counseling referrals if they found themselves having symptoms of post-traumatic stress disorder (PTSD)?

Our superintendent was unmoved. He said that the plan required that we should do CSID, and he told us a story about how in the mid-1990s the school had done a CSID procedure after a school incident and he thought that the procedure went fine. I then remembered an article I had read in the *New Yorker* magazine about the research done on CSID after the attacks of 9/11. I shared this article's findings with the superintendent and Mr. Calloway, saying that some recent research had showed that CSID could actually make people feel worse, particularly if they had a specific response to the traumatic event that wasn't shared by others in the group (Goopman, 2004). I said that I would be happy to retrieve that article if he wanted to read it. He looked at me and said, "No, I believe you. But if people want to know why we didn't do the crisis plan the way it was written, I'm going to need you to back me up!"

I didn't realize it then, but this was one of my first exposures to using EBP on the fly and making it work with the most powerful person in our district. I had created a question with my superintendent ("What are the potential outcomes of a CSID process in a school?" step 1 of the EBP process), taken some evidence (the studies on post-9/11 PTSD and CSID, step 2 of the EBP process) and applied it to my practice context, and designed an intervention (steps 3-5 of the EBP process).

In this case, I had actually chosen not to implement something, the debriefing. We did have a faculty meeting later that day, but not until we had already released a school letter describing the incident to teachers and parents and had given those directly affected a chance to talk with me and another school social worker in the district. The faculty meeting was the opposite of a debriefing; if anything, it was marked by the statement of

Mrs. Jones, who told everybody that she was fine and that she was eager to get back to work the next day. That seemed to satisfy the faculty; the rest of the meeting focused on the school's new math program.

Why Do EBP?

Throughout this book, there will be an effort to describe evidence as clearly, as accurately, and in as useful a manner as possible. This is more than just the goal of this book: It is in my view, the main reason why there aren't more mutually beneficial collaborations between practitioners and researchers. Both groups, in my view, tend to talk past each other (when they talk at all). And this isn't just my opinion; the study on the adoption of research-based interventions in schools reveals that very often researchers feel frustrated that practitioners don't "do" the interventions with adequate fidelity, whereas practitioners find the interventions designed and tested by researchers to be ultimately ineffective unless they can modify them to their own school contexts (Walker, 2004). Add to this sometimes frosty practitioner-researcher relationship the fact that many problems that present in schools don't have any solid empirical research done on them, and you have conditions that call out for a process that can help good research get into the hands of practitioners with minimal delay or difficulty (Raines, 2007).

This process, I believe, can happen in many different ways, but ultimately the process comes down to this: How can practitioners quickly and simply access current research and use it for the specific clients they serve? The EBP process, with its emphasis on school social workers collaborating with clients to design questions about the problems they face, finding and appraising the best available research, and implementing interventions on the basis of those research findings, presents a solid opportunity for school social workers to take evidence and turn it into useful practice interventions (Gibbs, 2003; Raines, 2004). In this book, the EBP process will be demonstrated in detail in the hope that EBP can become a straightforward and user-friendly way for school social workers to enhance their practice with their school clients.

How to Use This Book

This book is both a resource and an argument. The resource part will be easy to discern from the seven following chapters. In each chapter, I've drawn on case examples from my school practice experience to show the five-step EBP process model that forms the core of this volume. For each case I present, I will show how I did the following:

1. Co-created a question with my school client or clients
2. Investigated the empirical literature for the best available evidence (including consulting data sources within the school, like attendance or discipline records)
3. Critically appraised the evidence and shared my findings with my clients
4. Used the evidence to design an intervention that was in keeping with my school client's values and preferences
5. Evaluated the progress of the intervention and repeated the EBP process as needed.

All of the practice-related content in the following chapters will have both traditional APA-style references at the end of the book, and, where possible, online resources where readers can quickly get more information (and possibly even more current information than is possible in a published book).

In addition to providing resources for school social workers to use in their practices, this book also makes an argument. The argument is for a specific process to help enhance school social work practice itself. This process will be called, for this book, evidence-based practice (EBP). EBP has been referred to by social work scholars in the past decade as "evidence-informed practice," "evidenced-based practice," "best practice," and finally, "evidence-based practice" (Gibbs, 2003). Whatever the field ultimately settles on, this book will argue that a process of rigorous and collaborative interrogation of the best available evidence is a process that is in tune with our code of ethics (Gambrill, 2001). More than just reflecting our profession's code of ethics, I believe that EBP can ultimately benefit school clients in terms of improving school social workers' ability to engage clients in interventions and tailor those interventions to their specific needs more artfully. It will also allow school social workers to use their practice skills to apply this best available evidence to their own practice contexts and address the myriad challenges coming their way as practitioners (NCLB, outcomes-based education, and other efforts require to be more "research based").

This argument about EBP is already under way in many school social work settings, as administrators, state officials, and other regulatory groups require school social workers to document their effectiveness and, where indicated, use the preferred intervention strategy that schools consider "evidence-based." It is my hope that this book will help school social workers both operate creatively in this new practice environment and incorporate the better parts of the evidence-based ideas that have come to school social work in the past decade. I will be sharing empirical data from my own studies of school social work practice as well as case studies from my 15 years as a school social worker. Finally, through the work of the hundreds of school social workers I've helped train and supervise through Loyola's FSPP, I will be sharing how these ideas have played out in a diverse array of practice contexts. Let's get started . . .

2

A Short Chapter on EBP

EBP is defined for this book as a process of transparent, culturally sensitive, and evidence-informed practice that uses the best available empirical evidence to help clients solve their problems. In the context of a school, this EBP approach is particularly useful in helping parents, teachers, and students understand the myriad problems that present in schools. Though EBP is often caricatured as being rigid or dependent solely on manualized treatments, the EBP approach described in this book is more flexible and dynamic than the caricatures of EBP. Based on the work of social work scholars like Gambrill (2003) and Gibbs (2003), EBP in this book is characterized by the use of evidence to inform practice choices that ultimately are implemented by a collaboration between the social work practitioner and his/her client based on cultural, developmental, and ethical factors. This chapter will describe the basic tenets of this EBP approach and offer further resources for readers to consult to gain more knowledge about the different ways in which EBP is described in the literature.

This chapter will describe the advantages of using the EBP approach in school social work practice. Additionally, in the following chapters on individual student mental health problems, whole-school prevention programs, and family-based interventions, EBP resources and research findings will be shared with as much information as was available when the book was printed. This will help readers quickly access the best available research evidence to enhance their service to children, parents, and teachers in schools.

EBP is a movement that began in medicine (Sackett, Rosenberg, Gray, Haynes, & Richardson, 1996) and quickly spread into mental health disciplines including social work (Gibbs, 2003). The EBP movement in medicine and mental health has sought to equip health care providers and mental health practitioners with the best and most current empirical evidence to help them assist their patients/clients (Gilgun, 2005). In addition to using their experience and "practice wisdom," EBP challenges practitioners to collaborate with clients to solve their problems using interventions that emphasize client preferences and empirical evidence rather than interventions that emanate from the "expert" status of the practitioner. This call for empirically validated interventions has been reflected again and again in numerous social work, psychological, education, and special education regulations and policy statements that have called for practitioners to use evidence-based interventions in their work with children (Franklin, Harris, & Allen-Meares, 2006; Raines, 2007).

There are two other issues of accountability that EBP could help school social work educators begin to address: the mandates that all educators currently have to show adequate yearly progress (AYP) under the No Child Left Behind (NCLB) Act and the ethical debates currently swirling around the EBP movement in social work. All students (individualized education program [IEP] and regular education) are expected to demonstrate that they are making yearly progress toward curricular goals; IEP students have to also demonstrate annual progress in their academic/behavioral goals (Browder & Cooper-Duffy, 2003; NCLB, 2002). To do this, special educators (including school social workers) are expected to utilize the most empirically validated interventions. The Department of Education states in its executive summary of NCLB that educators need to be using research-based practices to help students learn and keep schools safe (NCLB, 2002).

Additional pressure to implement empirically based interventions for school social workers is coming from within the ranks of social work itself. The EBP movement (Gambrill, 2001) argues that social work practitioners need to move from an "authority-based" approach to their practice with clients to an approach that is more grounded in EBP and specific client concerns. Some social work researchers have openly wondered whether not using EBP and the empirically validated treatments available in the literature might constitute unethical practice (Thyer & Myers, 1999). How are school social workers responding to these new accountability pressures? Not enough is known about this important question; indeed, there has been no national survey of school social workers ever on these issues, and the most recent large-scale national survey of school social work practice is over 14 years old (Allen-Meares, 1994).

EBP as a Process

Although this EBP process can differ in small but significant ways for each client and problem context, the overall EBP process tends to follow similar steps based on Gibbs' (2003) conceptual framework and includes the following:

1. Identification of a problem that the client (and often in the case of children, the client system) wants to resolve and creation of an answerable question related to the problem that engages the interest of the client
2. Consultation of the evidence base by the school social worker (usually through online research databases) to identify the best available evidence to address the problem
3. Critical appraisal of the evidence in light of the rigor of the research and its applicability to the specific client's problem
4. Presentation of the evidence in the next session to the client in concise and developmentally appropriate language to help the school social worker and client make decisions about next steps to take, including interventions to implement to address the problem
5. Evaluation of the intervention plan undertaken and the consideration of either termination or a repeat of this five-step process to address another problem that has arisen in treatment (Gibbs, 2003; Raines, 2007).

This process is described visually in Figure 2.1.

My experience of using this method and teaching it to school social workers for the past 5 years has yielded evidence (via a content analysis) that most practitioners take three to five sessions to complete the above process, a timeframe that is manageable in the context of most schools where there is often time for longer-term treatment and assessment, particularly with students who have mandatory IEP minutes (Kelly, manuscript under review).

EBP in the Special Education Process: Helping Mr. Reyes Make the Call

Luis Reyes (not his real name), a sixth-grade Mexican American boy, wasn't coming to school much lately. He was hanging out at home mostly, playing

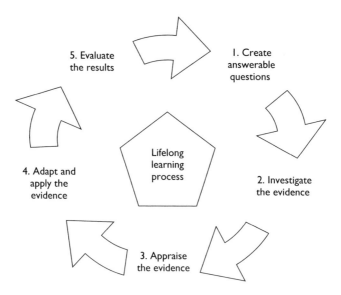

FIGURE 2.1. The Evidence-Based Practice Process. Source: Used with permission from Raines, J. (2008). *Evidence-based practice in school mental health: A primer for school social workers, psychologists, and counselors.* New York: Oxford University Press.

video games and telling his mother and father that he was "sick." He was rumored to be in one of our town's local street gangs, but it seemed unlikely to me because he seemed to stay home most of the time. (His mother, who was a stay-at-home mother, said he stayed in his room most of the time.) He had been in a few fights at our school, including one with a boy who was in another gang, so when I did a home visit to talk about getting him back to school, he told me that he "hated" our school because "nobody there watches your back, including the teachers."

Luis was missing a lot of school, and when he was at school, he was failing his classes. His reading teacher wondered if he had a learning disability and referred him to our special education team (called the student services team [SST]) to consider doing a case-study evaluation. The team readily agreed to pursue the evaluation, with our assistant principal adding that he thought Luis needed to be in a self-contained class that would address both his behavior and his learning problems. Though special education law requires the SST to defer placement discussion until an eligibility decision had been made, it seemed that my SST had already decided that Luis belonged in special education. Mr. and Mrs. Reyes signed the consent form to let us do the case study.

Domains and Demands of School Social Work Practice

In the parent interview portion of the case-study process, Luis' dad, Mr. Reyes, asked me what I thought about special education. I was unsure of what he meant and asked him to explain. He told me that he was a proud man who had built his own cleaning business after emigrating to Illinois from Mexico with only a fifth-grade education. He had three older children who had finished high school and were now either working with him or away at college. He saw Luis, his youngest, as a boy who just needed some extra help but worried that special education would be bad for him as it had been for one of his friend's sons. And then he asked me what turned out to be my first true EBP question (step 1 of the EBP process): What, he wanted to know, are the outcomes of Latino boys who go into special education, and what could be done instead of special education to help Luis? I told Mr. Reyes that I didn't know the answer to his question, but I would look into it and call him back with what I found out.

This was in 2002, and the Internet was nowhere near as developed as it is now for EBP resources. I did find some resources, however, to help answer Mr. Reyes' question, particularly a study entitled, "Special but Unequal: Race and Special Education" by Ladner and Hammons (available at http://www. edexcellence.net/foundation/topic/topic.cfm?topic_id=15). This study (part of step 2 of the EBP process) examined how special education placement differed in districts that were "majority-minority" and in those that were predominantly white, like the school that Luis was attending. The researchers found that race appeared to be a major factor in special education placement in white districts, and this reflected a general overrepresentation of minorities in special education (Ladner & Hammons, 2001). Outcomes from a major longitudinal survey (the National Longitudinal Transition Study [NLTS]) also indicated that students who had emotional and learning disabilities had adverse adult outcomes, though it wasn't clear whether special education placement had made their problems worse or helped blunt their impact (NLTS, 1993). I also found research on ways to use a new educational intervention, response to intervention (RTI), as a way to identify and treat students with learning problems without necessarily giving a special education label to these services (Fuchs & Fuchs, 1998). I thought that we could possibly design an intervention plan for Luis that didn't require special education, but I first wanted to see what Mr. Reyes thought of this (this appraisal of the evidence was part of step 3 of the EBP process).

I presented my findings on index cards, organizing them into key themes from the articles I had read (step 4 of the EBP process). I briefly described each piece of research I found and then gave the cards to Mr. Reyes and asked for his thoughts. Before he could answer, I noticed that he had started to cry. He said to me, "Nobody at Luis' school has ever given me anything to read before." He composed himself and told me that he would take the cards home and talk with his wife about them. The Reyes family did talk more and came back to our SST asking us to wait on any special education evaluation until we had tried some of the RTI ideas I had found about. Additionally, after talking more with the Reyes, I asked the team to delay the case study until I was able to get Luis screened and possibly treated for depression because I wondered whether this might be part of why he was staying inside all the time. The team reluctantly agreed to wait on the case-study process, and I was able to get the Reyes some mental health services that helped Luis get back to school and get more of his work done. Though he was still found to have a learning disability later in the school year, he was given only a period of resource help as opposed to the self-contained class that our SST had called for (step 5 of the EBP process).

Questions developed in the second step of the EBP process noted in the earlier section are called client-oriented practical evidence-search (COPES) questions and tend to cluster into three question categories (see Box 2.1 for more details) (Gibbs, 2003; Sackett et al., 1996). Because well-built COPES questions are central to an effective and efficient EBP process, interested readers are encouraged to consult the EBP resources listed at the end of this chapter before starting to use this process with clients.

EBP as a Process Versus Evidence-Based Practices: Two Contrasting Ways for School Social Workers to View Evidence

At times, the EBP process described in this book is incorrectly conflated with an EBP approach that emphasizes specific interventions over others because those interventions are considered "empirically validated" treatments that have been rigorously evaluated by intervention researchers. These interventions are typically chosen as being "evidence based" because the research supporting them used large sample sizes, control or comparison groups, and random assignment to treatment conditions (Gibbs, 2003; Sackett et al., 1996). Although evidence from such studies (usually referred to as randomized controlled trials [RCTs]) is useful and does often show strong evidence of intervention effectiveness, it is my view that such evidence is ultimately unlikely to have a significant impact if the critical

BOX 2.1 Client-Oriented Practical Evidence-Search (COPES) Questions: Examples of COPES Questions in School Social Work Practice

TYPE OF COPES QUESTION (BASED ON EXAMPLES FROM THE SCHOOL SOCIAL WORKERS IN THE FSPP)	TYPE OF CLIENT OR TYPE OF CLIENT PROBLEM	PARTICULAR INTERVENTION OR ISSUE BEING RESEARCHED VIA THE EBP PROCESS	INTENDED OUTCOMES OF INTERVENTION OR EBP LITERATURE SEARCH	EXAMPLES OF EBP SOURCES TO HELP ANSWER THIS QUESTION (ALL LISTED RESOURCES ARE FREE)
Effectiveness/ Prevention Questions	If students have symptoms of depression	Will small group counseling in the school setting	Be able to increase their coping skills and positively impact their academic achievement?	*Evidence-Based Mental Health* (U.K. journal with free abstracts of review of mental health intervention studies) http://ebmh.bmj.com/ Research in Practice (U.K. government site that assesses practice evidence for children and families) http://www.rip.org.uk/ SAMHSA's National Registry of Evidence-based Programs and Practices http://www.nrepp.samhsa.gov/

(continued)

	Type of client or type of client problem	Particular intervention or issue	Intended outcomes	
Descriptive Questions	If students are placed in special education classes for learning disabilities before third grade	What does longitudinal studies of educational outcomes for special education students	Say about their prospects for graduating high school and going to college?	U.S. Education Resources Information Center http://www.eric.ed.gov/ National Center for Education Research http://ies.ed.gov/ncer/
Assessment/Risk Questions	For schools that are concerned about school violence and bullying	What assessment tools have the schools used to effectively	Assess their school's overall risk for school violence and bullying and inform program development?	Early Warning, Timely Response: A Guide to Safe Schools U.S. federally supported report on school violence prevention http://www.ed.gov/about/offices/list/osers/osep/gtss.html University of Colorado Center for the Study and Prevention of Violence http://www.colorado.edu/cspv/index.html

Note. Each type of COPES question has been split across the columns "Type of client or type of client problem," "Particular intervention or issue," and "Intended outcomes" for clarity.

FSPP, Family and schools Partnership program; EBP, evidence-based practice.

components of client preference and school social worker "practice wisdom" are removed from the process and made subservient to the intervention itself. This view is supported by recent research on effective methods of training new social workers in the EBP process (Franklin et al., 2006; Raines, 2007). Additionally, it is clear from previous research reviews that the majority of mental health professionals aren't using the already "proven" empirically validated treatments for a variety of personal and context-specific reasons (Glasgow, Klesges, Dzewaltowski, Bull, & Estabrooks, 2004; McGlynn, Asch, & Adams, 2003; Walker & Gresham, 2003). Helping school social workers become more skilled at the EBP process seems particularly relevant, given the relative lack of solid empirical data on many school-based problems and the need for school social workers to view themselves as lifelong learners in the EBP process (Gambrill, 2001; Raines, 2004; Staudt et al., 2005).

One good way to assess school social workers' initial comfort with an EBP process involves exposing them to EBP researchers' understanding of evidence. To most practitioners, evidence isn't organized into the kind of hierarchy described by Raines (2008) in Figure 2.2. This hierarchy is however recognized by many researchers in the field of EBP as a way to assess the quality and rigor of intervention studies. Assessing the quality of evidence isn't just an idle parlor game for school social workers to play in their spare time: Helping school social workers become more skilled at the EBP process seems particularly relevant, given the relative lack of solid empirical data on many school-based problems and the need for school social workers to view themselves as lifelong learners in the EBP process (Gambrill, 2001; Raines, 2004; Staudt et al., 2005).

The EBP process advocated in this chapter provides several advantages for school social workers desiring to become more evidence based and increase their effectiveness in serving their school population. Advantages of using this EBP process approach include

1. the ability for school social workers to feel confident that they are using the best available evidence to help clients with their problems;
2. an increase in engagement between clients and school social workers as they work together collaboratively on client problems (many clients have come to their next EBP session eager to hear "what the evidence says");

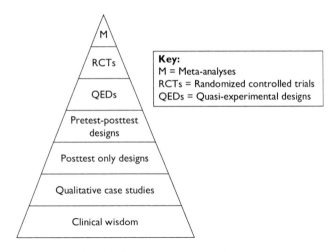

FIGURE 2.2. Hierarchy of Evidence. Source: Used with permission from Raines, J. (2008). *Evidence-based practice in school mental health: A primer for school social workers, psychologists, and counselors.* New York: Oxford University Press.

3. an enhancement in cultural competency skills for school social workers because the EBP process discussed here challenges practitioners to adapt empirical evidence to clients' cultural context.

All of these advantages are only tentative notions at this point, and more rhetorical than I would prefer, given the emphasis on solid empirical evidence being modeled in this book.

Additionally, a robust finding in the psychotherapy literature indicates that the therapist-client alliance and client strengths are more important for psychotherapy treatment effectiveness than specific techniques (Wampold, 2001). It appears that until further evidence is accumulated proving the specific ingredients of therapeutic interventions with children that make the most difference for most students, it will be necessary for practitioners to cultivate a degree of skepticism and critical thinking skills when presented with interventions that are called "best practices" or "proven" for treating childhood mental health disorders (for more ideas on how to critically appraise "best practice" evidence, see Figure 2.2). Although it is certainly possible that programs and interventions may someday become "universal best practices" for students with specific mental disorders (such as the two anxiety treatment programs I will outline in Chapter 5), the evidence base

Domains and Demands of School Social Work Practice

is still too thin to state categorically that specific interventions for childhood mental disorders are effective for most children most of the time, without also considering client preferences, client comorbidity factors (e.g., kids who are diagnosed with both attention-deficit hyperactivity disorder and anxiety), the skills of the practitioners delivering the intervention, and other socioeconomic/cultural/developmental variables that are often screened out of the intervention research process (Allen-Meares, 2007).

EBP Dos and Don'ts for School Social Workers New to the EBP Process

Do #1: Make the time. No new process will be adopted by any school social worker unless he or she has the skills to do the process, the tools to use those skills, and the time to put his or her new skills to work. Data from school social work surveys indicate that time is always at a premium for school social workers, who have huge caseloads and numerous unplanned demands on their time, mostly related to crisis intervention (Allen-Meares, 1994; Costin, 1969; Kelly, manuscript under review). The first step for school social workers to address this time crunch is to build EBP time into their schedules, possibly by making the EBP process a staff development goal with their principal or by offering to become the EBP coordinator for a team of school social workers (I will share more ideas on how to carve out EBP time in Chapter 8). There is limited evidence on how much EBP time is "enough" for school social workers to engage in an EBP process with their clients, but based on my trainings over the past 4 years on this topic, it appears that successful evidence-informed practitioners are able to devote at least a half a day a week to both conducting online searches for evidence and then translating that evidence into understandable material for their clients to use.

Do #2: Get the tools. EBP is only as good a process as the practitioner using it, and social work scholars have recently acknowledged the need to train social work students and practitioners

(continued)

---

better in how to conduct EBP database searches and critically appraise the available empirical evidence (Gibbs, 2003; Raines, 2004). The main tools currently available are online databases such as Social Work Abstracts and PsycINFO, summaries of systematic reviews of interventions from resources like the Cochrane and Campbell Collaborations, and federally funded resources like the What Works Clearinghouse (http://ies.ed.gov/ncee/wwc/) and the National Registry of Evidence-based Programs and Practices (http://www.nrepp.samhsa.gov). These resources contain abstracts of research articles and (in the case of Campbell and Cochrane) summaries of research findings that can give solid information to busy school social workers. For more in-depth information on how to devise a well-built question and find school social work-relevant EBP information, please consult another book in this Oxford series by James C. Raines, *Evidence-Based Practice in School Mental Health* (Raines, 2008).

Do #3: Find other evidence-informed colleagues to share with. There is a huge untapped source of information and talent all around us in schools—our colleagues, both in education and school social work. One of the most powerful applications of EBP ideas I witnessed involved a group of 12 school social workers in a suburban K-8 district who formed an "EBP study group." Given the huge time demands they all faced, they met for a day in August before school started to brainstorm eight topics related to their school social work practices for which they all wanted more information, and constructed EBP questions for each topic. They then proceeded to assign one topic each to two-person teams. Each team was responsible for appraising the research in that area and making a short presentation to the group at their monthly department meeting. The evidence the group presented was solidly grounded in the latest empirical literature, but it also adapted to the specific context of the school district and the strengths of the practitioners involved.

Don't #1: Don't let Google or Wikipedia do your EBP work for you. Given that so much information is so easily accessible through

(continued)

mega-search engines like Google, it is tempting to just type the specific topic or problem in and see what you find. There are several problems with this approach, not the least of which is that for many topics you will get thousands (if not millions) of responses, making it impossible to sort them out. Additionally, the first few responses will not be at the top because of their evidentiary rigor: Very often those web sites are themselves proprietary and are trying to sell a book or product that claims to effectively address the problem. A good piece of advice when faced with the temptation to use Google: Use Google Scholar instead, and then use the cites you find to search other more academically minded databases like PscyINFO or Social Work Abstracts to find the actual articles. Raines (2007) has another good tip if you do decide to consult Google: check out the URL. URLs that have a .gov or .edu are more likely to be Web sites that contain empirical evidence that has been in some ways peer reviewed and will likely be more reliable. However, for any Web site you encounter, it is essential that you be able to find out quickly and transparently the funders of the site, what evidence they are using to make their claims, and how their research was conducted. Any peer-reviewed web resource is required to make this information readily available (usually it's good to start with the "About" button on the organization's home page); some for-profit Web sites also are transparent about this information, but they aren't held to the same standards as the academic research-based sites.

Don't #2: Don't give up easily. One of the major problems in this whole field of connecting EBP resources to practitioners is a "digital divide" where researchers (mostly housed in higher education) have access to databases that aren't free and are thus inaccessible from home computers. There are many ways for school social workers to address this divide in their own work, but here are two that many of my former students have used:

1. See if your alumni status at your undergraduate or graduate university allows you to use their online resources;

(continued)

many alumni associations offer this as a perk, and having this access allows you to get to almost any of the major EBP resources that I've used to write this book.

2. Start first with the resources that are free (all the .gov Web sites are free, and many EBP databases at least provide free research summaries), get to know those well, and then work your way further into the other databases (for a sample of free EBP Web sites as of this publication, see Box 2.1).

Don't #3: Don't forget it's all about you (and your client). Even though evidence-appraisal skills are at the heart of doing the EBP process well, it doesn't mean that you have to become mini-research scientists to do EBP with your clients. Most of what you will do using the EBP process will look like what you already do well with your school clients: using your interpersonal skills to establish a good working relationship, incorporating contextual factors into your ideas of how best to intervene, and other things you already do. The new aspect of EBP will be that rather than relying exclusively on your past clinical experience to assist your clients, you will now be adding an extra layer to your work where you consult the evidence base in collaboration with them. You are still in charge of delivering the intervention, and no intervention will work unless you and your clients are willing participants in choosing and implementing it.

Myths About EBP: The Tyranny of Manuals, New Rigidities, and Other Caricatures of EBP

At this point, many readers will likely have plenty of questions about what EBP is and how they can go about implementing it more effectively in their school social work practice. Before sharing some case examples in Chapters 5 and 7 that show how I've used the EBP process to enhance my own practice with my school clients, it's important to at least raise (if not dispel) some of the myths about EBP that are out there in the practice community. These myths come from some of my experience teaching the EBP process to both new and seasoned practitioners and presenting some of my survey findings at academic conferences around the country in the past year. (Thanks also to James Raines for his insights on the caricatures of EBP.)

EBP Caricatures

EBP is just a fancy way of telling us, "do what's in the manual!" This idea is often cited by practitioners who are resistant to using empirical evidence to help inform their choice of practice interventions to clients. The concern is that by emphasizing research-based interventions, practitioners will just be required to follow standardized treatments with little room for creativity and client factors. This is a half-truth more than a myth because there are people in the fields of mental health and school-based interventions who are now pushing specific empirically validated treatments over all others (King & Heyne, 2000). However, the realities on the ground are that many problems in schools don't have empirically validated treatments and that many of our clients have too many co-occurring factors (e.g., poverty, comorbid psychiatric disorders, developmental issues) that make it hard to generalize the findings of clinical trials to their specific context. These complicating factors are what make EBP ultimately a collaborative and somewhat fluid process rather than one where manualized treatments are dominant.

Meet the new dogma, same as the old dogma: EBP is just a new way for us to impose our beliefs on our clients. Many school social workers first exposed to EBP get caught up in the process itself, feeling that they have to work harder to "do what I already know how to do." This notion, while certainly understandable when learning something new, is ultimately not the whole story. What makes the EBP process new for school social workers and not simply a new "dogma" is its emphasis of a collaborative process where school social workers' skills, their clients' goals, and the best available evidence all come together to help clients decide how to change their lives. As I've said earlier, this approach can only succeed with a client and school social worker collaborating on designing meaningful questions that they want to answer, finding that information out through the EBP process, and then applying that information to the specific client context.

As with any worker-client interaction, there are opportunities galore for spontaneity, brainstorm, and surprise. What my students tell me again and again about using this EBP process approach with their school clients is how it actually increases engagement with their clients, rather than make clients feel imposed upon: Clients feel flattered that their ideas and opinions are being taken seriously in coming up with the EBP question and are curious to know what evidence the school social worker has found.

One student of mine said that after she cocreated an EBP question with one of her students (who had attention-deficit hyperactivity disorder and had trouble making friends), the student stopped her in the hall all week saying, "Did you find out yet? Did you get the evidence yet?" That's the kind of engagement that most of us would love from our most challenging clients!

3

Surveying the Landscape of School Social Work Practice: What Are We Doing, and Why?

A century ago, three school districts in the northeast United States independently began hiring social workers to serve as outreach workers for truant students and to help those students increase their academic performance at school (Dupper, 2003). These first school social workers were called "visiting teachers," and many of their practice innovations (e.g., conducting home visits, leading classroom groups, consulting with teachers and principals) are still widely practiced in the field of school social work (School Social Work Association of America [SSWAA], 2005). Visiting teachers/school social workers formed their own professional association in 1921, and this association was merged into the National Association of Social Workers in 1955. Thanks in part to the increased emphasis on providing specialized educational services to students with special needs (highlighted by passage of a special education law Individuals with Disabilities Education Improvement Act [IDEA] in 1975), today there are school social workers in most states providing direct services to students, parents, and teachers (Dupper, 2003).

Answering the question of what school social workers are doing (and the related question, *why* are they doing what they're doing) is complicated by the fragmented and context-driven descriptions of what actually constitutes a "school social worker." In a recent survey of state education associations, only 20 states required a Master of Social Work (MSW) for certification of a school social worker, only 11 required a certification exam, and 19 required no specific degree to do school social work activities in a school (Altshuler,

2006). This is consistent with the findings from a recent survey of international school social work associations, in which out of 15 countries in industrialized and developing nations, most had no advanced training or certification requirements for school social workers (Huxtable, 2006). Beyond a handful of American states and countries, most school social workers worldwide seem to be fashioning their work role out of their own skills, their specific contexts, and whatever the local and state laws empower them to do. Answering the question of what school social workers do, while no less important to ask, is a daunting task indeed. What follows next is a consideration of how the "profession" of school social work has been constructed in one state and how Illinois has become a model in some ways for other states wanting to firmly establish school social work in both practice and policy. Additionally, a survey data just completed in 2006 on Illinois school social work practice will be shared to help contrast the state findings with other states developing their own school social work identities.

School Social Work Practice: Regional and National Survey Data, 1994-2007

It is important to know what school social workers all over the nation are doing in their practices today to build the "infrastructure of school social work practice" that Franklin (2001b) and other researchers have called for. This infrastructure is slowly being built by practitioners, clients, and researchers, as this book and others in the Oxford Workshop Series demonstrate. However, it is not always clear what strategies are being utilized by practitioners in the field, and how grounded in evidence-based practice (EBP) these intervention strategies are (Dupper, 2003; Franklin, Harris, & Allen-Meares, 2006; Frey & Dupper, 2005; Raines, 2004; Staudt et al., 2005). Although it is probably fair to speculate that school social workers nationally are like other social work subspecialties and have trouble keeping up with the latest research findings, it is unclear what school social work practitioners might want in terms of training or assistance to help their practices become more informed by an EBP process.

A gap presently exists in the literature here, as it is hard to say whether things have changed in school social work practice nationally since Allen-Meares' findings in 1994. Are school social workers utilizing the evidence-based interventions outlined in the literature to enhance their practices and improve their work in schools? If so, what are the EBPs that they are using most often? Is there any correlation between school social worker characteristics (i.e., demography, practice approach) and the utilization of EBPs? The relative lack of current information to answer this question made my Illinois study necessary as a first step because most data on school social work practice characteristics is over 10 years old. The growth in EBP, in social work practice in general and in school social work practice in particular, also makes the whole question about what school social workers "do" a significantly different one than what it was even in the late 1990s. New information that describes what school social workers are doing could make an important contribution to the school social work literature as school social work educators and policy makers (along with practitioners) try to define what school social work tasks will become most emphasized in the first part of the 21st century.

Allen-Meares (1994) collected and analyzed a national sample of school social workers to discern what work they typically focused on in their practices. She found that school social workers are largely focused on delivering individual and group mental health services to students, most often those with individualized education plans (IEPs) (Allen-Meares, 1994). School social workers described their work in this survey as a job having high autonomy, but also involving a high degree of pressure because of the direct-service demands. The stated hope by Allen-Meares that school social workers would be engaged in macro-level practice (or even school-wide prevention programming) was not something most survey respondents said they had time to do, a result she characterized as "disappointing" (Allen-Meares, 1994, p. 564). Clearly, though school social workers are heavily involved with the mandates of special education service delivery, large caseloads and multiple schools also appear to be major issues for school social workers nationwide, an issue that appears to be unchanged since the late 1960s (Allen-Meares, 1994; Costin, 1969).

Taking a cue from Franklin (2001b), who argued that school social work lacks an evidentiary "infrastructure" to base its claims on expert knowledge and effective practice, my Illinois survey project attempted to build a piece of that infrastructure in terms of learning more about Illinois school social work practice in 2006. It will be discussed in detail later in this chapter. Raines (2006), in his capacity as president of Illinois Association of School Social Workers (IASSW), told this researcher that without Illinois, most national school social work organizations would be severely reduced in their capacity to effect policy changes at the federal level (Raines, personal communication, May 15, 2006).

Unlike many other social workers, school social workers are very often supervised and evaluated by an administrator who is not a school social worker (Kelly, manuscript under review). School social workers therefore have to define what they do by being mindful of personnel expectations and norms more akin to teacher training than social worker training. Additionally, because many students are identified as needing social work services through their special education IEPs, a lot of school social workers' work is already defined for them: They are expected to be the "front-line" practitioners with some of the most complicated family and child mental health issues that a school community has. To help define what school social workers do, it is helpful to consider Perlstadt's definitions of discipline, practice, and profession:

> In addition, we should use the term *discipline* to refer to the development of abstract knowledge and instruction within and across academic institutions; the term *practice* to refer to the application of the knowledge system to diagnose, advise, counsel, intervene, and/or treat within an independent or entrepreneurial setting; and the term *profession* to refer to the umbrella covering both discipline and practice that fosters status and respect by establishing entrance examinations, practice standards, and codes of ethics to assure quality and protect the public.
>
> Perlstadt, 1998, p. 268

How school social workers view their practice and make decisions about what interventions to employ can be understood through a conceptual framework based on Perlstadt's definitions of discipline, practice, and profession, as well as Glisson's ideas about human service organizations (Glisson, 1992, 2000; Glisson & Hemmelgarn, 1998). A short introduction to these theories, which follow, may help explain why school social workers might have less "choice" than one might think. Focusing their time and energy on a full caseload of individual IEP students might be less of a personal practice choice than an expectation inherent to some of the very systems they practice within (Glisson & Hemmelgarn, 1998). The technology that all school social workers use to practice may be in large part determined by the structure that the profession has created for itself to survive over the past century. That is certainly the case for school social workers in Illinois, which has thrived in large part because of its ability to advocate successfully for a specific role in schools related to the delivery of special education social work services (Kelly, manuscript under review).

The Sociology of Professions and Its Application to School Social Work Practice

Sociologists of professions typically start with the knowledge base of a would-be profession to assess its level of professionalization (Abbott, 1988; MacDonald, 1995). Drawing upon Perlstadt's definition of a discipline in academia as "a development of abstract knowledge and instruction within and across academic institutions" (Perlstadt, 1998, p. 268), several sociologists of the professions have sought to explain how and why this abstract knowledge develops. To be successful as a discipline, a profession has to claim a knowledge base that is sufficiently abstract for it to perpetuate itself and carve out a niche that no other profession can fully address. Thus, the abstract and dense content of tax law requires accountants and tax lawyers to interpret it, x-rays require radiologists, and computer programs require IT professionals. As Abbott (1988) notes, "abstraction enables survival" as a profession (p. 30).

As the above examples indicate, professionals do not passively wait for their abstract knowledge base to collect and then simply rise to meet society's need to understand this new knowledge. As Larson notes in her influential study of American professionals, *The Rise of Professionalism* (1977), most successful professions embark on a "professional project" to establish their knowledge base and to control access to this knowledge base and to the ability to practice the skills required to use the knowledge base to help others. Her analysis challenged the initial view of functionalists like Carr-Saunders and Wilson (1933) and structuralists like Millerson (1964), who both argued that professions followed "natural" evolutions to become established and productive contributors to societal well-being; differences in professions' status could be attributed to their being further along in their evolutionary process (Abbott, 1988).

In states like Illinois, school social workers were able to establish their identity through skilled advocacy and a focus on establishing their knowledge base in relation to providing special education services (Morrison, 2004). The idea that school social workers alone could provide the related services that students with IEP required was not a given one when Illinois school social workers began organizing in the late 1960s. Rather, as Larson might argue, Illinois school social workers were able to establish their knowledge base in schools over time by creating specific licensure rules that required all school social workers to be certified by the state. In effect, Illinois school social workers got to the special education IEP mountain first and planted their flag. This process would be characterized by Larson and other thinkers like Freidson (1986) as evidence of a "monopolist" approach to establishing a professional identity. Larson and Freidson argue that professions are market-driven interest groups, motivated to expand their reach into new "markets" and to shore up their market share by controlling access to their knowledge base and skills (Larson, 1977).

With this lens, school social work knowledge itself, while obviously essential to enable the profession to claim its authority and establish dominance in certain niches, is not merely a natural by-product in a profession's search for truth. Instead professional knowledge is created, harnessed, and controlled by the many legal, professional, and organizational forces that professions marshal to build their power (Freidson, 1986). As will be demonstrated, this view of professions and the process of professionalization are particularly germane to this study of school social work, as the profession appears to be engaged in a constant effort to define, claim, and maintain jurisdiction over its abstract knowledge base.

The practice of professions, as Perlstadt (1998) and others like Abbott (1988) describe, is largely revealed in what the professions do: The "doing" of the profession is how power and status is maintained over other competing professions to be sure, but it is also how people outside the profession actually encounter the work of the professional. What's fascinating about school social work in this respect is that parents, students, and community members easily confuse us with other school-based mental health professionals such as school counselors and school psychologists, often having no idea about how our jobs might differ. Though school psychologists have more uniform requirements across most U.S. states, and school counselors require a master's in school counseling in 43 out of 50 states, there is little consensus nationally about how to best distinguish between these three seemingly related fields of school-based mental health (Altshuler, 2006). The differences between the three professions seem to have more to do with who have established themselves in certain regions of the country more than any specific claim to specialized knowledge.

School social workers might take a cue from a research-practitioner Web site devoted to ethical behavior by engineers. Though the professions differ greatly in their goals and their core technologies, the definition of what engineers do as practicing professionals mirrors what school social workers do. The definition is as follows:

> Profession: An occupation, the practice of which directly influences human well-being and requires mastery of a complex body of knowledge and specialized skills, requiring both formal education and practical experience.
>
> Case Western Reserve Engineering Center for Ethics, 2005

The school social work profession itself, as defined in the preceding text, requires direct action to help people (something school social workers do every day); it also acknowledges the need for formal education and practical experience, all of which is promoted by school social workers who have state certification standards and programs to fulfill those obligations (such as in Illinois through the master's-level Type 73 certification program and other states that require an MSW and specific school social work certification). Where school social work continues to remain ambiguous as a profession is in its ability to claim that its practitioners have a "mastery of a complex body of knowledge and specialized skills" (Case Western Reserve Engineering Center for Ethics, 2005). In a small way, the EBP process presented in this book may begin to enable school social workers nationwide to gain the skills to become evidence-informed practitioners who are able to make complex evidence understandable and relevant to their school clients.

The Illinois Example: How Did 3000+ School Social Workers Get Here?

The size and well-established history of school social work in Illinois made school social workers from this state a useful population to study to assess the state of school social work in 2006 and to help practitioners and leaders in school social work research and policy decide where to concentrate their energies in the coming decade. The SSWAA and the IASSW estimate that there are over 3000 school social workers in Illinois, making it the largest state concentration of school social workers next to New York State (Morrison, 2004; SSWAA, 2005). I have been training school social workers in the state for a decade, and I have seen a diversity of age, experience, and work environments that might indicate that school social workers are doing many more diverse activities in their schools than the typical IEP-driven framework that they have learned in their graduate training program. What is not known about these Illinois school social workers is what they are doing in their schools,

---

and whether their practice reflects the changing trends in prevention research, clinical practice, and educational policy. The Illinois State Board of Education (ISBE) made social/emotional learning a core of K-12 curricula, requiring school districts to design programs to meet specific social/emotional benchmarks (Collaborative on Social and Emotional Learning [CASEL], 2007). Many social work, psychology, and psychiatry researchers have demonstrated that systemic, school-wide programs for social/emotional learning and prevention are feasible to implement, provided schools have competent, well-trained professionals on site to implement the programs (Erickson, Mattaini, & McGuire, 2004; Mytton, Diguiseppi, Gough, Taylor, & Logan, 2002; Stevens, 1999; Tolan & Guerra, 1995). Additionally, school social workers are increasingly encouraged by researchers to form strategic partnerships with family and community agencies to enlarge their role and increase their effectiveness (Anderson-Butcher & Ashton, 2004; Astor, Benbenishty, & Marachi, 2003).

In Illinois, school social workers are mandated members of the school service personnel team, along with school psychologists, school counselors, speech pathologists, and other special education professionals (ISBE, 2005). In the 10 performance standards that the state of Illinois uses to evaluate competent school social workers, there is much obvious overlap with teachers, special educators, administrators, and other school mental health professionals in terms of the emphasis placed on understanding student and family needs, evaluating practice, and continuing to grow professionally (ISBE, 2005).

What is absent (or at least underplayed) in the standards themselves is the overwhelming reason that most Illinois school social workers have their positions to begin with: the special education provisions of IDEA requiring schools to have school social workers to assist in counseling and designing behavior management plans for students with IEPs (SSWAA, 2005). Illinois, more than most other states in the country, has embraced the IEP-based need for school social workers, making them charter members of the IEP team and requiring them to be at least part-time in every public school in Illinois (IASSW, 2005; SSWAA, 2005).

A major goal of this research was to discover how much the role of working primarily with students with IEPs has dictated the majority of work that school social workers in Illinois do on a day-to-day basis.

Demographic Information

Table 3.1 describes the demographics, professional experience, and work environment of the respondents. School social worker respondents

---

Domains and Demands of School Social Work Practice

practiced in all K-12 levels and in all community contexts. The majority of respondents were female (87.9%) and white (86.5%), reflecting national data from previous surveys (Allen-Meares, 1994; Costin, 1969). In terms of their professional experience, school social workers in Illinois are largely not practicing in other social work jobs before beginning their school social work career (67% of the respondents reported having no post-MSW experience before starting their work in schools). They were also working primarily in one school. One concern often described by school social workers in the field is their workload as related to number of schools they service and the possible constraints the workload might place on service delivery and practice choices. The majority (63%) reported working in one school only, 22% working in two, and the rest (15%) worked in three schools or more. Most schoolwork environments for the respondents were between 200 and 3500 students (89.6%), and all K-12 levels were represented, with most working in elementary schools (41.2%).

To address these above issues, respondents were asked to list all the interventions that they typically use in their school practices. Table 3.2 indicates that the overwhelming majority of respondents used individual and small group counseling most often in helping students. The other two treatment approaches of classroom groups, family therapy and joint sessions, though employed by many respondents, were rarely cited as the treatment option of choice for most situations. In Chapter 4, we will consider more closely what this data might say about the potential models of school social work practice nationally and offer some new ideas based on a synthesis of Frey and Dupper's clinical quadrant framework and the EBP process described in this book.

What Is the Nature of Contemporary Practice by School Social Workers? Specifically, to What Extent Does Practice Reflect Macro-Level Issues?

Illinois school social workers are overwhelmingly focused on the individual and small group treatment practice models to deliver their services, with over 88% saying that they utilize individual and small group interventions with students. Likewise, individual and small group interventions are the preferred interventions by school social workers in Illinois. Additionally, 41% of school social worker respondents reported that their practice is composed almost exclusively of students who have IEPs for school social work services, while 68% report devoting at least half of their time to serving students with IEPs. Overall, whether the students have IEPs or not, 62%

Table 3.1 Respondent Demographics, Professional Experience, and Work Environment

	RURAL (%)	URBAN (%)	SUBURBAN (%)	TOTAL (%)
Gender				
Male	5.8	12.4	14.6	12.1
Female	94.2	87.6	85.4	87.9
Race/Ethnicity				
African American	1.4	11.3	4.4	5.6
Asian American/Pacific Islander	1.4	2.3	0.6	1.4
Native American	0.6	0.6	0	0.2
White/European American	93.5	75.7	89.4	86.5
Hispanic/Latino	2.2	9.6	3.7	5
Other	1.4	0.6	1.9	1.3
Professional Experience in School Social Work				
Less than 4 years experience in school social work	24.6	16.9	24.1	22.3
Between 4 and 15 years	53.6	56.6	51.2	52.2
More than 15 years	18.1	24.2	23.4	22.8
Not presently employed as a school social worker	3.7	2.3	1.3	2.2

Number of Buildings Respondents Serve

One building	39.6	46	77.7	60.5
Two buildings	19.4	33	17.9	22.5
Three buildings	17.3	14.2	2.5	9
Four buildings or more	23.7	6.8	1.9	8

Primary Grade Levels Respondents Serve

Early childhood	5.1	5.1	2.8	3.9
Elementary school	42	42.1	40.4	41.2
Junior high/middle school	13.8	14.2	24.1	19
High school	15.9	22.2	23.8	21.9
Other school configurations*	23.2	16.5	8.8	14

Size of Respondent Schools

Fewer than 200 students	5.8	5.7	4.4	5
201-1000	62.3	54.6	63.8	60.8
1001-3500	26.8	35.8	27.5	29.6
More than 3500	2.6	2	2.2	2.2
Don't know/not sure	2.5	1.8	2.1	2.4

Note. All figures are percentages and based on data collected from 637 participants who completed the School Social Work Survey. Data are missing for two cases for professional experience, and for four cases for the number of buildings, grade levels, and size of respondent schools.
* Other school configurations include K-12 schools, alternative schools, and private schools.

Table 3.2 Illinois School Social Workers' Practice Choices

Interventions Used With Students	
Individual counseling	96%
Group counseling	89%
Classroom groups	70%
Family therapy	17%
Joint sessions with students and teachers	40%
Interventions Used Most Often	
Most often used individual counseling	55%
Most often used group counseling	37%
Other (classroom groups, family therapy, and joint teacher and student sessions)	8%

Note. All Illinois figures are percentages based on 820 participants who completed the School Social Work Survey. Percentages do not add up to 100%, as respondents could select more than one choice for each question.

of Illinois school social workers report that they serve between 20 and 50 students per week in their schools.

These study findings do not reflect the empirical literature on effective preventive, systemic practice in schools. Reviews of the literature indicate that this level of service delivery is likely concentrated on "indicator" interventions with select students who already exhibit behavioral/emotional problems, but not with students who might be prevented from developing problems by early intervention (Allen-Meares, 2004; Erickson, Mattaini, & McGuire, 2005; Frey & Dupper, 2005; Newsome, 2005). Most survey respondents are spending the majority of their time seeing a small number of students who have been already identified by an IEP team, and thus may not have the time to devote to more prevention-based interventions. Additionally, despite their possible intentions to do prevention-oriented or school-wide interventions, the numbers of students served and the high percentage of students served with IEPs seem to indicate that Illinois school social workers are not engaged in practice that serves their whole-school population.

How Are School Social Workers Influenced by Contemporary Best Practice Literature for School Social Work?

Almost all (99%) the school social workers reported having at least adequate access to a computer for their work, and 80% reported that they thought they had adequate access to online databases and research that would allow them to stay current with the latest interventions from EBP. On analyzing the data from section two of the survey that dealt with case vignettes and potential interventions, it's clear that a majority of school social worker respondents report using at least one or two interventions that have strong empirical backing to deal with common student and school problems. However, of the eight vignettes in which "research the latest treatment methods using online databases" was an option, school social workers chose that option never more than 31% of the time. For six of the eight vignettes, fewer than 20% of the school social workers reported that they would consult online databases for help in designing interventions to help their student clients. Though 80% reported feeling that they have the access to such resources, fewer than 30% appeared to view consistently those online databases as helpful resources to consult. This finding is consistent with other research on practitioner's low use of research-based literature to inform their practice decisions (Glasgow et al., 2004).

How Are Practice Choices Influenced by Organizational and Institutional Factors in Their Work Settings?

School social workers' organizational contexts are understandably diverse, given the many different regions of the country and grade level configurations. Still, some consistent patterns emerged from the Illinois survey data that might provide some data to compare to other state and national survey data. Ninety percent of respondents worked for one public school district, while 7.6% reported working for special education cooperatives that served multiple public school districts. In terms of their schools' grade levels, school social worker respondents practiced across all potential grade levels.

One important organizational context that has been identified in the literature is the degree to which school social workers collaborate with teachers and use that collaboration to enhance their effectiveness (Allen-Meares, 2004; Frey & Dupper, 2005). Several Illinois survey questions dealt with the connection between school social workers and teachers in the school setting. Forty percent of school social worker respondents cited teachers as their primary referral source (second only to the special education IEP team), and 60% of respondents reported consulting with teachers at least two times a week on their students. Twenty-nine percent said they meet with teachers every day to consult with them on their students.

Most respondents reported feeling they had enough administrative, secretarial, and technological support to do their jobs well. Respondents overall felt that their schools were well-run and positive places to work. A significant majority (60%) had worked for at least five principals over their careers and most of the respondents (67%) said that most of their principals understood and supported their work. What is not clear from these findings is whether principals support the work their school social workers do and want them to do additional activities (like prevention or other more systemic interventions).

Organizational factors such as principal support, positive school climate, or heavy IEP paperwork loads did not appear to be associated with school social workers expanding their work to include more non-IEP students. The only areas where statistically significant associations were found were between higher teacher-school social worker interaction and more joint teacher-student sessions, and low IEP paperwork demands (i.e., fewer than 6 hours a week) and classroom group interventions. Though almost all respondents reported seeing at least a few non-IEP students in their schools, it's not clear from this study that positive organizational factors are significantly associated with individual respondent's non-IEP caseloads.

From these results and the above survey data, it appears that a majority of Illinois school social workers are pleased with their working environments. Though it is encouraging to see that so many school social workers perceive their environments positively, their overall perceptions of good principal support, good morale, and fair school rules are not associated with their having more involvement with delivering school social workers services to non-IEP students or doing more prevention-oriented practice. School social workers who reported having fewer than 6 hours a week of IEP paperwork also tended to report conducting classroom groups but did not report doing family therapy or joint sessions with students and teachers. The only other hypothesis that had a strong association was the one that sought to test an association between high levels of teacher consultation and use of teacher-student joint sessions.

School social work in Illinois in 2006 appears to be characterized by only sporadic examples of the clinical quadrants framework that Frey and Dupper (2005) discuss in their theoretical paper on school social work practice (more information on Frey and Dupper's ideas is contained in Chapter 4). There is, to be sure, some evidence from this survey that the more systemic practice that Frey and Dupper called for is happening in Illinois. Over 30% of respondents reported that they had used parent surveys and evening parent groups to reach out to disengaged parents; 59% said that they had instituted school-wide conflict resolution programs to help prevent conflicts before they began. Seventy percent said that they had used classroom groups to address student needs; 40% had used teacher-student joint sessions; and 17% had used family therapy in their school setting. All three of these interventions have shown some success in helping students develop resilience and prevent future behavioral and emotional problems (Early & Vonk, 2001; Franklin, Harris, & Allen-Meares, 2006). Still, none of the above interventions was the intervention of choice for more than 6% of the entire sample. The larger conceptual framework that Frey and Dupper envision is a long way away from becoming the intervention mode of choice for the majority of Illinois school social workers.

Summary of Illinois Findings

Data from the survey indicate that Illinois school social workers are very satisfied with their work (over 93% say they'd become school social workers all over again), but a significant number of them struggle with how to effectively serve students using the latest EBPs. Additionally, many of them practice within a special education framework that limits their time to engage in an EBP process to find, design, and implement evidence-based interventions that might significantly impact the entire student body, or to conduct family-based programming that might help strengthen parents' connections to their child's school. In this way, school social work in Illinois appears to be based on the "core technology" of special education IEP mandates and individual and small group counseling, rather than any of the recent practice innovations of the past two decades. Based on these findings, the need for more knowledge about the EBP process and its application in Illinois' school social work context is clear. In attempting to define the profession, it's important to remember that one of its key ingredients is the institutional context of the school—a context that itself is shaped by educational mandates like the recent federal education legislation No Child Left Behind (NCLB) and the 30-year federal tradition of IDEA. This issue seems particularly germane to the study, given that the organizational contexts school social workers practice in do not seem to facilitate the active embrace and implementation of many evidence-based interventions (Allen-Meares, 1993; Franklin, 2001b; Glisson, 1992).

Finally, in constructing itself as a profession, Illinois school social workers have worked to establish "market dominance" over the domain of IEP-related counseling services, and they have largely succeeded (Freidson, 1986;

IASSW, 2005; Larson, 1977). School social workers claim unique (exclusive) skills and training (IASSW, 2005). But it appears that they have instead created specific requirements for gaining access to the profession that might also be claimed by other school-based special education and mental health professionals like school counselors or school psychologists, if those professions had been able to claim legal jurisdiction over these requirements (Abbott, 1988; Larson, 1977). It is possible to point to some developments that suggest this exclusivity is contested. For example, in Oak Park, Illinois, the high school decided several years ago that the IEP-service function of school social work could be "out-sourced" to agencies and private practitioners rather than having a large (and more expensive) school social work staff deliver the IEP services. Those outside clinicians came from social work, but also from psychology, professional counseling, and substance abuse counseling backgrounds, making school social worker's claim to exclusivity over those services irrelevant in this instance (J. Williams, personal communication, January 10, 2005).

Although it's impossible to generalize these survey findings beyond Illinois, given that much of what this survey says about the highly IEP-based nature of school social work in Illinois, it is essential to have comparative data from school social workers in other states to see if their practice models might be more effective than that in Illinois. The overwhelming majority of Illinois school social workers appear to view their job through two lenses: IEP-mandated school social workers' minutes and long-term individual and small group counseling interventions. Both these lenses are not the norm in other states like Texas where most school social workers are based in community mental health agencies and deliver targeted brief treatment (Franklin & Gerlach, 2006), Missouri where brief treatment and crisis intervention are more prevalent (Jonson-Reid et al., 2004), or Ohio where brief treatment and truancy interventions are more common (Newsome, 2004). Indeed, in his survey of state boards of education, Torres (1998) found that school social work practice varied widely across regions, with some states emphasizing more consultative and training roles (Hawaii, Kansas, and Minnesota, among 10 other states), while others like Illinois were more focused on IEP tasks (Alabama, Connecticut, and Wisconsin, among 14 other states).

One major issue that we will address in Chapter 7 on increasing school safety is the persistent issue of school violence. Thanks to the work of numerous prevention researchers over the past 20 years and the financial commitment of federal agencies like the Office of Safe and Drug-Free Schools, we now have a number of promising (and even some effective) interventions to prevent and reduce school violence that have been shown to have positive effects in diverse school contexts (Elliot, 1998).

A national survey of school social workers by Astor and his colleagues (1998) revealed demographic information similar to my survey, but also revealed troubling findings about school social workers' sense of personal safety in their school positions. Particularly in inner-city schools, Astor and his colleagues found that 71% of the school social workers employed in inner-city high schools reported feeling fearful for their personal safety, and that this might have impacted how they, and others in more "safe" perceived neighborhoods, decided to implement violence prevention programming (Astor, Behre, Wallace, & Fravil, 1998). Additionally, though their study was confined to finding out about interventions employed to address school violence, Astor's team found that some of the individual and small group counseling interventions were dominant despite the clear need for more parent-oriented and community-based interventions (Astor et al., 1998).

In addition to dealing with school violence prevention and the potential impact of violence on the actual types of school social work services provided, the other major study of school social work practice related to school social workers' perceived cultural competence. Teasley et al. (2005) conducted an exploratory survey of school social workers using a convenience sample of school social workers and regional and national conferences. The results of this survey match what I found in my own survey in terms of school social worker demographics: In Teasley's survey sample, school social workers were on average in their 40s, and had been a school social worker for an average of 9 years (Teasley, Baffour, & Tyson, 2005). Another interesting finding from the study was that years of experience and advanced licensure were associated with higher perceived levels of cultural competence (Teasley et al., 2005).

Jonson-Reid (2004) and her team's study also merits attention, even though it was not a survey of a whole state or national sample. Her team's work represents one of the most detailed attempts by school social work researchers to describe what a group of eight school social workers (four full-time and four interns) did with their time. Over the course of 1 year in a suburban K-12 school district in St. Louis in 1998-1999, Jonson-Reid and her team created a management information system (MIS) with the school social workers there to track the referrals made to them, the nature of those referrals (presenting problems), and the year-end outcomes of the students referred (graduation, resolution of problem, disciplinary actions taken against the students referred). Her sample of referrals for school social work assistance ($n = 911$) was more focused on family issues, suspected abuse and neglect, and attendance than on the self-reported issues the school social workers from my study of Illinois focused their energy on. Additionally, most of the students received school social workers services over the course of 3 months, a contrast to the IEP-based model in Illinois, where 41% of school social workers reported seeing most of their students for an entire year.

Interestingly, the sample in the Missouri school district was mostly composed of regular education students: The students with IEPs received services from a special education-only school social work team who were consequently not included in this study, possibly because they were not "of" the school and provided the services as part of a special education coop-erative. Only 11% of the entire sample involved "assessment/collaboration with special education staff," a dramatic contrast to Illinois, where 41% of all initial referrals for school social work services originated in the IEP process (Jonson-Reid et al., 2004, p. 13). Despite the seeming opportunity to serve more regular education students in more prevention-oriented and systemic programs, it is unclear from Jonson-Reid's data how much of her school social workers group did any of the work. (Perhaps most significantly, the question of diverse practice approaches and multilevel practice interven-tions never appears in her analysis of the study itself or the limitations of her approach to understanding what constitutes school social work *cases*. The assumption from the beginning of this study is that school social work services solely involve individual and small group counseling for students presenting with mental health problems.)

Finally, despite the lack of IEP mandates in this school district the eight school social workers in the study gave services to 250 students a month, averaging 31 students per school social worker—a similar figure to that reported by 62% of the Illinois respondents. From the descriptions in this study, it seems that most of those services were delivered in traditional ways: No classroom groups, family therapy, or teacher-student sessions are men-tioned in the study. To be fair to the authors, it bears pointing out that Jonson-Reid et al. are mostly counting referral and attendance data and not trying to discern what practice interventions these eight school social work-ers used to serve their students (Jonson-Reid et al., 2004). Seemingly, despite a removal of a major obstacle to delivering different practice interventions (minimal IEP mandates and paperwork burdens), this group of school social workers appeared to favor the same traditional school social work practice that the majority of Illinois school social workers do.

How Do Organizational Factors Affect What School Social Workers Do? Further Thoughts on Preferred Versus Available Technology in Schools

The final research question for this chapter, how organizational and institutional factors might affect practice choices, is a relatively new one in school social work research. Earlier, survey research had asked school social workers to rank tasks according to their importance (Allen-Meares, 1977, 1994; Costin, 1969) and found that administrative tasks, home-school liaison, educational counseling with children, facilitating and advocating families' use of community resources, and leadership and policymaking were the top five job factors or skills considered important for entry-level school social workers to possess (Allen-Meares, 2004, p. 98). Allen-Meares (1994) found that most of the tasks that school social workers actually performed were mandated, that is, IEP related, though she doesn't extend that information to delve into what specific practice choices these school social workers made to cope with those mandates.

What makes the Illinois study both an amplification of Allen-Meares and Costin's earlier work and an extension of it is that the study focused specifically on what school social workers say they do with their caseload, not just how large or small or IEP related their caseload is. That is to say, are school social workers using interventions that are indicated by their specific client population's needs and the latest empirical evidence of effective treatments, or are they more likely to simply use the "core technology" that has been shaped to fit the constraints of the particular school context they practice within?

First, some overview comments based on the evidence of this study: School context, supportive or not, "healthy" or dysfunctional, IEP-heavy or not, had no statistically significant association with whether or not Illinois school social workers chose to implement "cutting-edge" clinical interventions (available technology) like classroom groups, family therapy, and joint teacher/student sessions. There was also no statistically significant association between school social workers who reported relatively low weekly IEP paperwork loads and those who implemented classroom groups, family therapy, and joint teacher-student sessions. To the contrary, significant majorities of school social workers said that they had good support from their principals, saw their schools as positive and fair places, and even thought that the staff morale of their institutions was strong. Significant majorities also reported feeling well supported by school secretaries and having enough computer access and office space to do their jobs properly. According to the hypotheses underlying this study's third research question (summarized in Table 3.3), all of these organizational and institutional factors should have made more of a difference. After all, if the school cultures aren't holding school social workers back from employing a wider range of available practice interventions (let alone working on more systemic, whole-school levels), then further investigation is needed to find out what the barriers are for school social workers.

One immediate question could be asked of this finding: So what? Aren't IEP students the neediest of the needy, and aren't school social workers supposed to be in the business of helping the most in need? On top of that question, school social workers in Illinois may be intensively rooted in IEP-based services, but it could be argued that this has been a good thing for the profession's stability and growth (SSWAA, 2005). Finally, initial pilot data from our national survey indicates that other school social workers still define their professional identity through a clinical lens, but with more attention paid to serving students without IEPs (Kelly, manuscript under review). The key to understanding the dynamics of the professionalization underlying school social work in Illinois may lie in the ideas about professions overstating their knowledge base and unique skills. The sociologist of professions Freidson was keenly aware of the paradox of professions institutionalizing themselves without adequate practice frameworks to support their knowledge base, saying that without being "down at the level of everyday human experience" (1986, p. xi), a professions' knowledge base lacked real substance.

Ironically, though school social workers in Illinois can claim to be the nearly exclusive provider of a mandated service to some of the neediest children in Illinois schools, there is almost no evidence to support their contention that they have any particular "core technology" that is uniquely suited to addressing these students' needs. (There was no large-or even medium-sized intervention study based in Illinois schools involving IEP students that could be found for this study's review of related literature.) If anything, the evidence from this survey data indicates that most of what Illinois school social workers do for these students most of the time is not particularly

Table 3.3 Hypotheses on Organizational Factors and Their Impact on School Social Work Practice Choices

	RESULTS	SIGNIFICANCE
1. Perceived principal support is associated with more school social work respondents reporting increased work with non-IEP students	0.17	NS
$n = 636$		
2. Perception of positive school climate is associated with more work serving non-IEP students	School morale: 2.66 School rules: 1.85	NS NS
$n = 636$		
3. High level of school social worker-teacher consultation is associated with more use of joint counseling sessions with teachers and students together	20.26	*
$n = 798$		
4. School social workers who report doing 5 hours or less of IEP paperwork are associated with using classroom groups, family therapy, and joint teacher/student sessions more often than school social workers who report doing 6 hours or more of IEP paperwork	Classroom groups: 3.80 Family therapy: 0.01 Joint sessions: 0.47	** NS NS
$n = 748$		

Note. All χ^2 tests had one degree of freedom. NS for each χ^2 test varied due to missing cases, and NS for each test are noted in the table. NS, Nonsignificant; *, $P < .001$; **, $P < .05$.

rooted in EBP (Early & Vonk, 2001; Franklin, Allen-Meares, & Harris, 2006; Newsome, 2004). What is highly rooted in the practice choices of Illinois school social workers, however, are the practice contexts that arrive with every Illinois mandated IEP student: namely, the assumption that school social workers are to provide weekly, ongoing long-term treatment for students with IEPs, perhaps indefinitely.

Given that school social workers (in Illinois and elsewhere) have not yet developed an abstract body of knowledge that is IEP-specific (e.g., showing how their long-term treatment increases academic achievement or decreases chronic mental health problems like attention deficit hyperactivity disorder [ADHD] or depression), it is unclear how much of a professional identity Illinois school social workers can lay claim to, and how much are they beginning to resemble the tradespeople who are brought in to do "part of the job" at the IEP staffing and to provide service to the students identified there.

At this point, there is no indication that there is a statewide challenge requiring Illinois school social workers to answer this provocative challenge. The state ISBE standards refer to competent school social workers practice that involves evaluating practice and demonstrating effectiveness, but demonstrating and measuring practice outcomes are not cornerstones of the standards used to evaluate school social workers in Illinois (ISBE, 2005). However, it seems unlikely that it will be long before the requirements of "highly qualified" educators to use scientific educational practices as required in the federal mandates of NCLB make their presence felt in the work environments of Illinois school social workers. One neighbor state (Indiana) is anticipating such a challenge to school social workers' professional identity and is trying to define itself before outside forces define them (Constable & Alvarez, 2006).

Presently, Illinois appears to be maintaining its identity and its remarkable growth as a haven for school social work. But could the good times of professionally protected roles and minimal demands for accountability be coming to an end? The twin forces of NCLB in education and EBP in social work generally might create a "perfect storm" that disrupts and seriously challenges the relatively comfortable place Illinois school social workers find themselves. And if so, what will be the response of Illinois' school social workers? In my view, it is unclear whether budget-conscious administrators and school boards uninformed about the nuances of school social work practice accept the premise that IASSW promotes school social workers

Domains and Demands of School Social Work Practice

who have unique knowledge and skills that require their presence in every Illinois school.

Conclusion

Recently, many school mental health experts (in social work, psychology, and pediatrics) have called for more integrated, systemic mental health delivery systems in schools to help reach the millions of students believed to be suffering from undiagnosed and untreated mental health issues (Erickson et al., 2004; Franklin et al., 2006; Mytton et al., 2002; NASW, 2002). Recent school social work scholarship has focused on the need for school social workers to take the lead in designing and implementing school-wide prevention and mental health promotion programs, for example, in the area of violence prevention (Astor et al., 2003; Erickson et al., 2004). A recent content analysis of school social work intervention research has shown the need to develop coherent and relevant practice guidelines for school social workers informed by actual practitioner feedback and input (Staudt et al., 2005).

Despite these calls for systemic and integrated practice and practice guidelines, the most recent national survey of school social work tasks (Allen-Meares, 1994) indicated that most school social workers are delivering individual and group counseling services to a specific population (students with special education labels under IEPs), and crisis intervention. Consequently, most school social workers appear to be devoting little of their time to prevention programming or other examples of systemic work due to their high caseloads of students with previously identified special education needs or ever-increasing crisis intervention needs (Allen-Meares, 1994). My Illinois survey project found that even after 12 years, Allen-Meares' findings are still accurate in describing the majority of school social work practice choices in Illinois. This survey data is consistent with other recent state and national studies of school social work practice (Astor et al., 1998; Jonson-Reid et al., 2004; Kelly, manuscript under review).

4

■ ■ ■

Where to Intervene, and How? The Debate Over the Best Treatment Options for School Social Workers to Use

School social work enters its second century as a profession still bedeviled by confusion about its central mission. Are school social workers meant to be "in-house" clinicians providing services to kids in need, or are they meant to be involved in program development to enhance the social/emotional learning of all students in a school? How much time should they devote to serving whole families, or consulting with teachers? Whatever school social workers claim to be doing in their schools, it's clear that they have to prove that they are effective in doing it. The demands of federal legislation like No Child Left Behind (NCLB) and state requirements for certification are making it increasingly necessary that school social workers demonstrate that they are highly qualified school-based mental health professionals who can demonstrate outcomes that impact school "bottom line" issues like student achievement, attendance, and behavior. Rather than recoil from this pressure, school social workers can utilize the skills of evidence-based practice (EBP) to help them enhance both their effectiveness and their knowledge of interventions that work to help students, teachers, and parents in school contexts at all levels of the system.

Numerous recent school social work articles have called for practitioners to adopt a multilevel approach to school-based intervention (Anderson-Butcher et al., 2007; Franklin & Gerlach, 2006; Franklin, 2001b; Massat, Ornstein, & Moses, 2006). A version of this multilevel approach, summarized by Frey and Dupper in their 2005 article "A Broader Conceptual

Approach to Clinical Practice for the 21st Century" calls on practitioners to be able to decide whether the individual student, family, classroom, or even whole school needs to be the starting point for a particular school social work intervention.

The results from the surveys summarized in the last chapter reflect how organizational factors may shape the landscape of school practice sometimes, it might be argued, at the expense of serving other students in need. Evidence in this chapter will also show that many school social workers are choosing to focus on individual students and their psychopathology even when the empirical evidence shows that intervening at a family or classroom level might be more effective. The 100-year-old debate about choosing the right approach to intervention in schools will be summarized, with the new wrinkle of EBP and Frey and Dupper's clinical quadrant framework added to the mix as possible ways for school social workers to choose more adroitly both their specific intervention and the best level in which to deliver the intervention.

Frey and Dupper argue that school social workers are always going to need to do individual and small group counseling; they are instead seeking to expand the notion of what other "clients" school social workers might serve beyond the traditional notions of students with presenting mental health problems. They maintain that in prevention-oriented work, systemic practice including community organization, parent outreach, and in-service trainings of teachers is just as essential to school social workers being effective in serving the needs of children as individual and small group counseling (Frey & Dupper, 2005).

Leading school social work researchers have sounded a call for more research on effective school social work interventions (Dupper, 2003; Franklin, 2001a; Franklin, Harris, & Allen-Meares, 2006; Newsome, 2004). Despite these calls, the field seems to suffer from a persistent role confusion, as school social workers struggle to be recognized as uniquely effective school-based mental health practitioners (Franklin, 2004; Raines, 2004; Staudt et al., 2005). Recent attention to the social-emotional needs of students in the national media has underlined the potential leadership role that prevention-oriented school social workers might have if they were able to reconfigure their role within the school environment (Shriver & Weissberg, 2005).

More than ever school social workers need theoretical models and intervention methods that are grounded in research methods and strategies for increasing their accountability and commitment toward EBPs. Yet, the field of school social work, similar to other areas of school-based policy and practices, has lagged behind in producing research-based practices (Allen-Meares, 2007). At this juncture in history, the school social workers have been called upon to assemble their knowledge and to educate themselves on what is needed to produce better research-based practices.

Mirroring the complexity of the practice field that we learned about in Chapter 3, school social work scholars have leveled multiple critiques of student-focused casework methods that are not grounded in any specific empirical method or approach. Questions have been raised not only about the extent of empirical support for these methods, but also about their potential to exacerbate problematic labeling of students in schools. Yet, few of these discussions move the field to find a new way to conceptualize practices outside the boxes of micro versus mezzo and macro practices to match client problems with the most well-suited intervention or to integrate newer practices and EBPs into the work of school social workers by offering methodological solutions to study school social work practice in the context of schools. This chapter will offer some thoughts about how to use two frameworks (the clinical quadrant framework from Frey and Dupper and the EBP process model described by Gambrill [2001], Gibbs [2003], and Raines [2004]) to think more deliberately (and it is hoped) more effectively about which school social work interventions to implement in which situation.

Several school social work scholars have suggested that this "drift" to casework is also shaped by a limited scholarly knowledge base that only partially captures the actual complexity of the practice field (Allen-Meares, 1994; Constable, 2006; Kelly, manuscript under review; Staudt et al., 2005). Ultimately, a brief review of the literature on school social work practice choices, their school contexts, and their attempts to establish professional identities on the basis of specific roles and tasks suggests that historical and school organizational factors represent potentially important explanatory mechanisms and, as such, map the ecology of school social work practice. The ideas in the previous chapter on the sociology of professions and Glisson's (1992) ideas about professional technology in the human services articulate how and why schools and school-related processes must be understood as a central mechanism shaping school social work practitioners and their practice choices, particularly the choices they make about the levels at which they think they need to intervene in most often.

School-Based Mental Health Interventions: If We're School-Based Clinicians, How Are Our "Clients" Doing?

Although school social workers and other prevention specialists may be eager to address the many social, emotional, and academic needs of students, there are only initial signs that school-based interventions are actually effective in addressing student problems. Early and Vonk (2001) found that school social workers had demonstrated some small-scale empirical effectiveness addressing student problems, but that further study was warranted, as the sample sizes of studies were so small and little longitudinal research had been undertaken. Likewise, the researchers at the Collaborative for Academic, Social, and Emotional Learning (CASEL) argue for both individual and group social-emotional programmatic interventions as well as school-wide programs. However, they note that the current state of empirical research is still emerging and more study is needed to demonstrate what approaches (if any) have long-term positive effects on students' social and emotional learning (Greenberg et al., 2003; Weissberg & Durlak, 2007).

A recently completed meta-analysis of school social work intervention studies (Kim & Franklin, manuscript under review) found 14 studies that addressed at least one of the following three areas of student behavior: academic outcomes (e.g., attendance, grade point average), behavior that was externalizing (e.g., impulsivity, and physical and verbal aggression), and behavior that was internalizing (e.g., depression, anxiety). In their meta-analysis, an unconditional random effects model and positive medium effect sizes for all three student behavior areas were covered. Though the number of studies is still small, it does reflect well on school social work as a role that can and does make a difference on the main issues that school social workers are asked to address. As we shall see in Chapter 5, the need for school social workers to address externalizing and internalizing student problems specifically is pronounced, and there is a great need for more research on school-based interventions on these issues that can be considered evidence based.

The small number of school social work-specific intervention studies in the literature is particularly concerning, given that school social workers are often the "go-to" person for the most at-risk students in the school. Those students are often the ones with individualized education plans (IEPs), and the lack of more intervention data on how best to help these children address their disabilities and their other problems is sobering. In Chapter 6, we will look more closely at the response to intervention (RTI) movement in education and will analyze its potential as a tool for school social workers to use to develop and implement an EBP process with students who are academically and behaviorally at risk.

What About Prevention? The Rise of the 3-Tier Model of Intervention

In addition to RTI, the notion of intervening at different levels of a population has gained increasing traction in a variety of education- and mental health-related fields, including school-based mental health (Gresham, 2004). The 3-tier model is reflected in Figure 4.1 and it reflects a growing research base that asks policy makers and practitioners to think more clearly about what different populations in a particular context (in our case, a school context) might need in terms of a specific intervention or instructional strategy. For example, as we will see in Chapter 7, there are bullying-prevention programs that are targeted at all three tiers of intervention: general lessons on conflict resolution and peer mediation programs for all students (tier 1 or the primary or universal level), conflict-resolution groups and social skills training for students who have had one bullying incident, either as a bully or as a victim of bullying (tier 2 or the secondary or targeted level), and

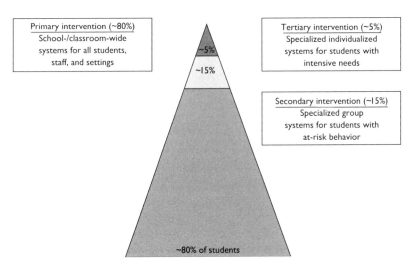

FIGURE 4.1. Continuum of School-wide Support. Source: Adapted from "What is School-Wide PBS?" OSEP Technical Assistance Center on Positive Behavioral Interventions and Supports. Accessed at http://www.pbis.org/schoolwide.htm

Where to Intervene, and How?   59

family therapy and individual behavioral contracts for students who have had numerous incidents of bullying or being victimized (tier 3 or the tertiary or the indicator level).

The mental health prevention literature to date has been largely concerned with programs to decrease specific behavior problems at-risk students have (Massat, Ornstein, & Moses, 2006) rather than tackling head-on the two crucial issues for at-risk students of low academic achievement and special education referral (interestingly, those tasks are increasingly being brought under the purview of RTI, an intervention system that is not always led or even staffed by school-based mental health personnel, but instead is often staffed by special educators or reading specialists). This move toward more prevention work has clearly been heightened by the NCLB act, which expects educators to be able to demonstrate they can improve student outcomes in both regular education and special education settings, or face possible consequences for their schools. For the first time, the federal government is requiring schools to disaggregate their data to show how much their students in special education are learning and how their learning compares to those students in regular education (NCLB, 2002). Whether it comes through the efforts of a dropout prevention program or an RTI-based program, schools are increasingly expecting their entire faculty to think more about preventing behaviors that lead to unsafe schools and low-achievement for at-risk students (Raines, 2006).

Still, school social workers, in many parts of the country at least, seem to be embracing the very individual treatment-based clinical model that contrasts so sharply with the move towards whole-school intervention and prevention going on in the school-based mental health literature (Franklin & Gerlach, 2006).

Survey data obtained from a convenience sample of school social workers (n = 44) at the School Social Work Association of America (SSWAA) conference in Orlando, April 2007, indicated that these school social workers largely practiced in individual and small group contexts. Additionally, over half of them served mostly students with IEPs and had limited time to devote to prevention work in their school social work practices. One interesting contrast between the Illinois sample and the SSWAA sample was the preference of the latter sample for classroom groups, family therapy, and teacher/student sessions as the treatment modality they used most often. (See Table 4.1 for more information on the SSWAA sample and the Illinois survey of practice choices.)

Table 4.1 School Social Workers' Practice Choices, Illinois and Nationally

	ILLINOIS (%)	SSWAA SAMPLE (%)
Interventions Used With Students		
Individual counseling	96	95
Group counseling	89	79.5
Classroom groups	70	45.5
Family therapy	17	43.2
Joint sessions with students and teachers	40	54.5
Interventions Used Most Often		
Most often used individual counseling	55	41
Most often used group counseling	37	21
Other (classroom groups, family therapy, and joint teacher and student sessions)	8	33

Note. All Illinois figures are percentages based on 820 participants who completed the school social work survey. Percentages do not add up to 100%, as respondents could select more than one choice for each question.
SSWAA figures are based on a convenience sample $n = 44$ of school social workers who attended the SSWAA National Conference in Orlando, Florida in April 2007.
SSWAA, School Social Work Association of America.

Reclaiming and Expanding the Clinical Roots of Our Work: The Clinical Quadrant Framework

Figure 4.2 shows the clinical quadrant framework (Frey & Dupper, 2005) and lists examples of interventions within each quadrant that school social workers might choose to employ in each quadrant. On first glance, many school social workers will recognize the bulk of their work likely to be contained in quadrant C. This quadrant includes individual/group counseling, family therapy, home visits, and most components of the special education/IEP evaluation process for a student being considered for special education services. In Chapter 5, I will offer examples of ways to use the EBP process to garner the best available evidence to help school social workers make decisions about interventions in all the quadrants.

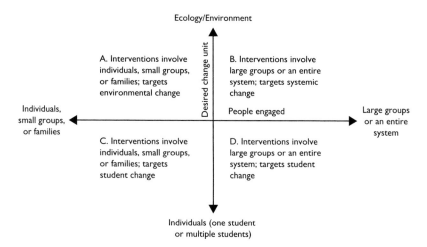

FIGURE 4.2. Clinical Quadrant. Source: Frey, A. & Dupper, D. (2005). A broader conceptual approach to clinical practice for the 21st century. *Children & Schools,* 27(1), p. 36.

One of the problematic aspects of school social workers conducting an EBP process and applying it to their school social work practices is the relative lack of macro-level practice interventions that have been rigorously tested and measured for school social work practice (Franklin et al., 2006). This is because the literature on school social work interventions in schools is still struggling to integrate either the clinical quadrant framework outlined here or the 3-tier model of prevention. Part of what makes the clinical quadrant framework attractive here is that it acknowledges that many school social workers view their jobs through a clinical lens and are trying to ultimately use clinical skills (interviewing, active listening, showing empathy) to impact their school at both micro and macro levels.

What follows is a description of the types of programs/interventions for each quadrant, with some ideas about potential school social work skills that might be helpful in operating within the particular quadrant. I also offer a potential synthesis of the clinical quadrant framework with the EBP process outlined in Chapter 2 to help practitioners think first about where best to intervene and then about how to find and use the best available evidence to intervene effectively.

As will be shown in this chapter, there are rarely shortages of ways to operate in this (or any other) clinical quadrant. Many of the ideas I will share are based on my own practice experience, the literature on effective and promising intervention strategies, or a combination of both. There will be many ideas I'm sure school social workers will have as they read the rest of this book about things they have done for a specific problem or an intervention they've been meaning to try the next chance they get. That's great, and I'm happy if this book gets some creative thinking going. However, the main difficulty for many school social workers isn't thinking up a new way to approach a problem, but finding the time to implement it well. My Illinois survey data showed that most respondents were spending at least a day a week working on IEP paperwork, significantly limiting the time many of them had to try new interventions.

The challenge, as with all interventions, is to know where best to start. Many school contexts and roles within those contexts can be inherently reactive, driven by crisis intervention and shifting priorities from teachers, parents, and school administrators. As indicated in the description of each of these quadrants, the first step involves carving out time (both psychically and literally) to step back from the torrent of school problems all school social workers deal with and to focus on the problems with an eye toward the "bigger picture."

Quadrant A: Intervening With Individuals, Small Groups, or Families to Promote Change in the School Environment

School social workers intervene in this quadrant to help specific target populations just as they do in quadrant C, but they are also concerned that these targeted interventions will influence the school's overall responsiveness to student, family, and community needs. Examples of interventions in this quadrant include

1. working with teachers to set up class meetings to discuss issues in the classroom and enhance the classroom climate;
2. teaming up with teachers to use newsletters and introductory letters to welcome students and parents to the school and to model the teacher's cultural competence and openness;
3. developing a "bookmarks" program where school social workers and teachers share information about student developmental milestones and help parents see what is developmentally appropriate for their child and what might need further investigation;

4. serving on RTI teams, helping parents and students to have voice in the process and to assist in case managing the RTI process (for more information on RTI, see Chapter 6).

Gary Bowen (Woolley & Bowen, 2007), a leading school social work researcher at the University of North Carolina-Chapel Hill, has written extensively about the interaction between student achievement and the student's affective investment in his/her school. By thinking about how to make schools places where students and their parents feel invested and welcome, school social workers increase the home-school connection and are able to assess more clearly what the school student population's needs are to plan future interventions in this quadrant and the other three. (A highly useful assessment tool is Jack Richman and Bowen's School Success Profile [SSP], www.schoolsuccessonline.com; for more information on how to use SSP to conduct needs assessments and plan interventions, see Bowen & Richman [2001]).

Quadrant B: Interventions Targeting Change Within a Whole School System, Involving Working With Large Populations or Serving in Policy-Making Roles

From some pilot work I've done for a future national school social work survey, this is the least-active quadrant for most school social workers, with most of us devoting no more than 10% of our time to it (Kelly, manuscript under review). This quadrant in some ways may not even seem "clinical" in the narrow conception of psychological interventions, though I think it's a crucial aspect of our work to improve outcomes for our school clients. Examples of interventions in this quadrant include

1. serving as services coordinator for a community school, helping bring health, mental health, and recreational and even vocational services into the school for students and parents to use;
2. writing grants to bring additional services to the school district, for example, seeking Office of Safe and Drug-Free School grant money to bring gang-prevention programming to the school district;
3. chairing the school's crisis committee to examine how the school can use the best available evidence to prevent crises and respond to crises that do happen;

4. initiating a series of "house meetings" with parents to hear their concerns about the school and to build more of a home-school connection with traditionally "hard-to-reach" parents.

One of the challenges in this quadrant involves a combination of our own personal views of our capacities and the structural constraints of many of our school social work roles. In the last decade of my work in the Family and School Partnerships Program (FSPP) at Loyola, I have heard again and again from our trainees how they felt very comfortable doing "clinical" work in their offices and working one-on-one with students, but felt less sure about how to assume more public leadership roles in their buildings. Additionally, when we do have job descriptions for our school social work positions, they may be written in ways that explicitly privilege the work done directly with students, with the work in quadrant B seeming more the province of administrators or department heads.

It is understandable that quadrant B might be the least-utilized quadrant in many school social workers' practices. However, that doesn't mean that it isn't important or that targeted involvement in this quadrant can't help school social workers have a huge impact on their school community. Since many school social workers are expected to serve on committees in their schools, either at a school or district level, this may be the best place for them to start looking at what student/family issues they could significantly influence using an EBP process. This will help their committee members think about ways to help implement programs or interventions that might change the whole school or school district in positive ways.

Quadrant C: Individual, Small Group, and Family Therapy Interventions Designed to Target Specific Client Psychological and Behavioral Changes

For many school social workers, school social work really *lives* in the intimate and direct work they do with clients. Indeed, this is where the term "clinical quadrant" may be seen to apply most clearly, as it involves school social workers doing direct observation and treatment of clients in their schools. The challenge here, as will be discussed more thoroughly in Chapter 5, is how to use the EBP process to make sure that the interventions that school social workers select for this quadrant are based on client preferences and goals and the best available evidence they have access to at that time. With more than 400 schools of psychotherapy (Hubble, Duncan, & Miller, 1999), and a host of treatment workshop and program brochures claiming to be "effective" that arrive in our school mailboxes weekly, the problem here will never have anything to do with helping students in quadrant C, rather it will involve doing something that is likely to be effective, or at the very least, not harmful to our clients.

Quadrant D: Interventions That Target Whole School Populations but Focus on Helping Individual Students Change

This quadrant should be a natural extension of school social workers' direct service work, as schools are full of predictable and constant mental health/behavioral/developmental issues that they deal with each year. For example, as a school social worker in a K-5 building, I could pretty much set my calendar by when I would start to get calls from parents of third graders asking me about what had happened to their child's social relationships. It was usually in early third grade, and they would tell me that suddenly their child was telling them that they weren't "popular" with certain kids and that a former best friend wasn't interested in them anymore. Beyond the individual issues these students might have had, there was clearly something developmentally afoot here. After a few years of working with each case individually, I decided to design and implement friendship and social skills groups in each of the third-grade classrooms for girls and boys to talk about how to handle conflicts that arise between friends and how to discern what made for a good friend. I based my work on some of the social skills training interventions I will outline in Chapter 5. Although the calls from parents didn't stop completely, I found that doing a tier-2 intervention (i.e., targeting students at risk for a problem and using the 3-tier framework of intervention I mentioned earlier) helped our third graders learn how to make friends and manage the inevitable developmental conflicts more smoothly. It also normalized the process for teachers, who could refer back to our classroom group lessons when they were helping mediate student conflicts.

This is just one of many quadrant D interventions I've used over the years. Some others include

1. designing a depression prevention program for adolescents using interventions derived from positive psychology (more on how I did this program in Chapter 7);
2. implementing a parent group for all parents who had children in the school's special education program, describing

strategies for coping with their student's disabilities and managing their child's behavior at home;

3. starting a "sportsmanship intramural league" for K-5 students, where no score is kept based on points, goals, or runs, but instead each competing classroom team gives themselves a 1-10 score on the basis of how much good sportsmanship they show to each other and the opposing team.

The challenge for this quadrant is, like all the others, in finding the time to step back and assess your population, and then using the EBP process to find the best available evidence to design interventions that have a good chance of being effective. Another particular challenge here is the unfortunate tendency school social workers may have in their work roles to become isolated and disengaged from the natural leaders of the school community. I was always the only school social worker in my building, and often the only professional specifically dedicated to providing counseling and mental health support to students. Along with the natural drift I always felt towards quadrant C interventions, it was easy to forget that the other quadrants aren't possible without our using our community organizing and facilitator skills to get others involved in helping us. Personally, I found this work to be the most far-reaching and gratifying work I did in my 15 years as a school social worker. Without my school's natural leaders (children, teachers, parents, administrators) assisting me, I couldn't have done any of the above quadrant D interventions; more important, I wouldn't have been able to see the positive effects of these interventions carry on past my specific time with the targeted student populations. The power of interventions that utilize shared ideas about how students can change their schools (and their lives) is truly a beautiful thing to behold, but you can't do it alone.

Synthesizing the Quadrants and the EBP Process: Notes on an Emerging Model

As part of the Family and Schools Partnership Program faculty at Loyola, I've long been preoccupied with how to help school social workers adapt good research to their specific practice contexts. This is no small task, and many other researchers are also concerned about bridging this research-practice divide (Gambrill, 2001; Glasgow et al., 2004). What I hope to give you in this section are some practical ideas about how to integrate the clinical quadrant framework and the EBP process we discussed in Chapter 2.

Figure 4.3 shows the decision pathway that synthesizes the quadrant model and the EBP process. To distill this emerging model, the two most important facets of this model for school social workers are to know their school population and to then know how to find the best available evidence to help them serve that population. Within any potential problem, it may be necessary to intervene at multiple levels, for example, giving a student individual counseling for friendship problems, leading a classroom group in her class, and consulting with the principal about a friends-social skills curriculum for the whole school to consider adopting. That's fine, as long as school social workers are ready to bring an EBP process to all those levels and evaluate those intervention's impacts. More realistically, they will likely want to start at one level and then move on to others as they accumulate more information and client input into the EBP questions they want to explore.

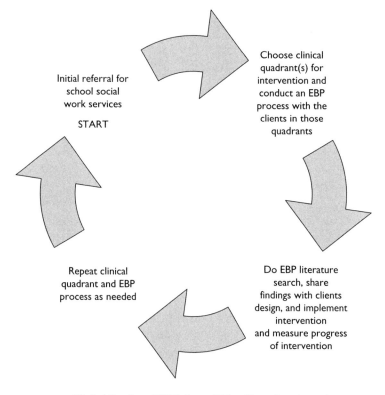

FIGURE 4.3. Clinical Quadrant/EBP Pathway. EBP, evidence-based practice.

The appeal of this process is that it is flexible to allow school social workers to both react to current needs and look ahead to future problems that they might want to address. It also allows school social workers to maintain the best parts of their individual clinical work with clients and creatively think about ways to enlarge their roles in schools without losing their clinical focus.

A Final Note: The School's Most Important Client

Using the clinical quadrant framework to expand and enhance one's school social work practice can be an exciting and rewarding process. I look back at my favorite school social work interventions and the outcomes I'm most proud of and can see that I was thinking in terms of the clinical quadrants well before I read about it in *Children & Schools*. I hope that at this point in reading this book, school social workers are able to be thinking about all the times they've designed effective interventions for their school by combining aspects of the different quadrants. With the EBP process and resources discussed throughout this book, they will be able to use the best available evidence to make the most impact they can on their school community.

But any description of interventions and levels of intervention would be incomplete without an acknowledgment of the most important client in almost every school: the principal. A burgeoning literature on principal leadership is pointing to the strong influence that effective principals have on school climate, parent engagement, faculty morale, and student achievement (Andrews & Soder, 1987; Leithwood & Janzi, 1999). Good principals (and conversely, incompetent principals) set the tone for a school and can be ultimately the most important ingredient of a school making a significant turn-around. Many large urban school districts have recognized the importance that strong principal leadership can have on low-achieving schools, and have started "principal academy" partnerships with local schools of education to address the shortage of principal candidates in urban schools (Peterson, 2002).

Whether school social workers feel that their principals are strong leaders or not, they are likely going to need to make them one of their primary clients as they try to move their practice to one based more on the EBP process and the clinical quadrants. The nature of principal-school social worker collaboration is one that is woefully understudied, but my experience leading trainings and consultation groups at Loyola's FSPP indicate that majority of our most dynamic school social workers figured out to work with (or in some cases, around) their principals. I'll share more ideas on how to make a school more grounded in an EBP process in Chapter 8, including ideas about how to bring a principal into the EBP process outlined in this book.

5

Why Johnny Needs Help: The Most Common Clinical Issues School Social Workers Face

In the Illinois survey sample, school social workers reported dealing with social skills deficits, attention-deficit hyperactivity disorder (ADHD), and anxiety most often in their practices. These referral problems can all be successfully addressed using the EBP process. Using case examples and summaries of the best available evidence, this chapter will describe ways to use an EBP approach to successfully engage school clients (students, teachers, and parents) in implementing interventions at both micro and macro levels to address these clinical issues. Both treatments rooted in the EBP process described in this book, as well as more manualized treatments that have empirical support of effectiveness, will be described in this chapter to show the diversity of current intervention "evidence" and how it can be appraised and then implemented by school social workers.

For this chapter, I am adopting the EBP process that I detailed in Chapter 3 and locating it on specific problems that many school social workers told me they work with every day. In the spirit of "practicing what I preach," I want to detail from the outset about how I went about compiling the evidence that you will find described in the sections and tables that follow, making clear what choices I made in appraising the evidence base for each of the five major problems identified from my survey data. It's my hope that although this approach may be new to some or even most of my readers, by the end of this book, they will feel comfortable interacting with evidence in ways that emphasize clarity, accuracy, and usefulness

Table 5.1 Most Common Referral Reasons for School Social Work Services

	RURAL (%)	URBAN (%)	SUBURBAN (%)	TOTAL (%)
Social skills deficits	90.7	80.2	89.1	85
Problems related to students having atten-tion-deficit disorder	69.1	57.1	62.3	61
Student anxiety	56.8	42.4	69.5	60
Students not following classroom rules	70.5	66.1	62.6	59
Bullying (either acting as the bully or being victimized by others)	62.6	51.4	65.1	56

Note. All figures are percentages and based on data collected from 821 participants who completed the Illinois School Social Work Survey in 2006.
Percentages do not add up to 100%, as respondents could select more than one choice for each question.

of evidence for their work with actual clients in their school context. Table 5.1 outlines the major reasons for referrals for school social work services from the Illinois sample, and will form the basis for three EBP process examples in this chapter.

For each of the three mini-reviews I conducted a search of the literature using the following three major resources:

1. Three online databases, the National Registry of Evidence-based Programs and Practices (located at http://nrepp. samhsa.gov/find.asp), the U.S. Department of Education's *What Works Clearinghouse* (located at http://www.what-works.ed.gov/), and the University of Colorado's Center for the Study and Prevention of Violence Blueprints for Violence Prevention site (located at http://www.colorado.edu/cspv/blueprints/). These three sites were chosen because they are related to the three top areas identified by my survey, they are all largely grounded in school-based research, and they

demonstrate high standards for evaluating the potential effectiveness of interventions.

2. The four major school social work textbooks, all of which had presumably updated findings through 2005, the year before they were last published. The books I used were:

Allen-Meares, P. (2007). *Social work services in schools* (5th ed.). Boston: Allyn & Bacon.

Constable, R., Massat, C., McDonald, S., & Flynn, J. P. (2006). *School social work: Practice, policy and research* (6th ed.). Chicago: Lyceum Books.

Dupper, D. (2003). *School social work: Skills and interventions for effective practice*. Hoboken, NJ: Wiley.

Franklin, C., Harris, M., & Allen-Meares, P. (2006). *School services sourcebook*. New York: Oxford University Press.

All of them had some content reviewing research on the key referral problems identified in my survey.

3. I then used an electronic database search of the following common article databases using keyword search terms based on the tools from leading social work EBP resources (Gibbs, 2003). For example, for social skills deficits, I used the search terms, "effective social skills programs schools" and "social skills training school interventions" to collect my articles. Because the textbooks I was consulting had updated resources through 2005, I searched from January 2006 to August 2007. The databases I searched were contained in a helpful "mega-database" tool entitled qUICsearch based at the University of Illinois-Chicago, which allowed me to search EBM Reviews (a collection of systematic reviews from the Cochrane and Campbell Collaborations, among others), PsycINFO, Academic Search Premier (EBSCO), and Social Work Abstracts all at once.

I collected all the hits I found for each topic and read the articles for each one, looking for studies that met the following criteria, based on some of the criteria from the Blueprints for Violence Prevention and Stone and Gambrill's review of school social work textbooks (2007):

1. The study had an experimental or quasi-experimental design with a control or comparison group, and a sample size that allowed for statistical power (check rubrics for how to best say this part).
2. Subjects for the study were randomly assigned to each treatment condition and the method for making the random assignment was clearly spelled out in the text of the article.
3. The study had been conducted in a school setting.
4. Findings from the study had sustained treatment effects after 6-month follow-up.
5. The study had materials that could be easily accessed for implementation with clear instructions on how to get training in the intervention at a reasonable cost (defined as somewhere below $1000, my pupil personnel department's typical professional development budget when I was practicing full-time in a school).

If all of the above criteria were met, I judged the intervention to be "effective." If any combination of the above criteria was met, I judged the intervention to be "promising." If none of the criteria was met, but the intervention had some research support (single-subject designs, a pre- and posttest with no control group), I listed the intervention as "emerging." Though it was hard for any study or intervention to meet the above criteria, I wanted to work with rigorous criteria to evaluate the studies for this book. This is in part because the nature of evidence itself is constantly evolving and changing, and making any statements about interventions that are "effective" is at best solid only for the timeframe when this EBP process was conducted. Additionally, I wanted to show that while few interventions could be considered "effective" by this standard, and thus generalizable to a school setting and relatively easy to adopt and implement, many others might have elements that were "promising" or "emerging" that might ultimately be the best evidence available at this time. Unlike a bell curve image, there was no presumption that there would be "effective" interventions unless they met the criteria. Let's go appraising, shall we? (Box 5.1).

BOX 5.1 Appraising Research Findings in the EBP Process: Some Key Questions

1. How did the researcher gather the information? (methodology of study, measures used)
2. What was the sample for the study, and how similar is it to the client you're working with for the Client-Oriented Practical Evidence Search (COPES) question? Was the sample large enough to have statistical power to show statistically significant results?
3. What are the results of the study? How significant are the results (the study's effect size)?
4. How rigorous was the study (consult Figure 2.2 for the hierarchy of evidence to help assess the study's research design and its level of rigor)?
5. If the findings were significant and relevant to your client's COPES question, how feasible would it be to apply the intervention in your school setting? Is there additional training required to deliver the intervention, and if so, what is the cost of that training?

All the above questions should be readily available in the text of a well-designed research study or meta-analysis.

Sources: Gibbs, L. (2003). *Evidence-based practice for the helping professions.* New York: Brooks/Cole; Sackett, D. L., Rosenberg, W. M. C., Gray, J. A. M., Haynes, R. B., & Richardson, W. D. (1996). Evidence-based medicine: What it is and what it isn't. *British Medical Journal, 312*, 71-72.

Social Skills Deficits
Step 1: Creating an Answerable Question

Social skills were clearly on the mind of many survey respondents in Illinois, with over 85% identifying social skills as a referral reason for school social work services. A quick perusal of the current literature on school-based interventions reveals a perplexing fact about social skills training: There is little agreement about what constitutes social skills, and researchers and practitioners unfortunately use the term in so many diverse ways as to render it close to meaningless (Caldarella & Merrell, 1997). This is perhaps an unfortunate and unintended outcome of a fragmented research agenda and diverse researchers from the fields of social work, psychology, psychiatry, and public health have all been working for several decades now to design interventions to help students learn social skills (Dupper, 2006). One robust finding from the longitudinal research on students who have adverse outcomes as adolescents and/or young adults is that they often lack good social skills, for example, meaningful and healthy friendships and the ability to manage conflicts with peers. These social skills problems increase their risk for having poor outcomes (Dupper, 2006; Gresham, 2002). For the purposes of this chapter, I'm defining social skills on the basis of the typology offered by Caldarella and Merrell (1997), highlighting the ability to work cooperatively, develop and maintain interpersonal relationships with peers and adults, and manage conflicts that arise in normal school situations.

For my EBP process, I've chosen the question, "What are effective interventions for increasing student social skills in a school setting, compared to school-based treatment as usual or control group conditions?"

Steps 2 and 3: Investigating and Appraising the Evidence

Fortunately, as Table 5.2 shows, some programs and interventions qualify as "effective" and "promising" for school social workers wishing to increase students' social skills. These interventions often operate on multiple levels, involving students in individual treatment, small group counseling, classroom groups, and even whole school programming. However, a crucial caveat to all this research on school-based social skills training, particularly for young children, is that the effects gained by a school-based intervention could be more effective when coupled with family and parent interventions (Webster-Stratton & Taylor, 2001).

Step 4: Adapting and Applying the Evidence

Ideally, becoming skilled in teaching students social skills should allow school social workers to increase their reach as practitioners to almost every part of the school community. As will be discussed in detail in Chapter 7, schools are always interested in finding ways to increase academic achievement. A recent meta-analysis of social-emotional learning (SEL) programming interventions showed that students who received good SEL programming achieved better grades and scored higher on standardized tests (CASEL, 2007).

According to my own survey data and other views of school social work practice, individual and small group work are two of the major ways by which most school social workers deliver most of their services to students, particularly ones who have trouble with social skills (Frey & Dupper, 2005; Allen-Meares, 1994). This can be certainly understood in the context of how social skills problems might present themselves, for example, a specific third-grade boy is having trouble making friends, or a group of seventh-grade girls is struggling to maintain friendships in the light of rumors and bullying. However, it is worth asking whether all the individual and small group work necessarily generalizes to the larger social context these students inhabit, and whether the skills they learn are maintained in those environments. For this reason, it is important to utilize the clinical quadrant framework I outlined in Chapter 4 to consider whether a number of social skills needs might be best met by addressing the entire classroom, or even by devoting time as a school community to a system of positive behavioral supports that model and teach good social skills for all students. While the clinical quadrants and the 3-tier models of intervention offer plenty of promise to help school social workers intervene at many different levels to help students and families, as with this example of social skills, the research base is still thin in terms of allowing us to call any social skills program comprehensive across all possible levels of intervention (Webster-Stratton & Taylor, 2001).

Step 5: Evaluating the Results of the Social Skills Intervention

Like many respondents to my survey, when I was practicing I had many referrals for social skills deficits during my time as a school social worker. One student I had (call him Matt) was constantly using his words ineffectively in class. I say ineffectively because he was a good talker, just not always good at using the right words to solve his problems. He would often talk himself deeper into trouble with teachers and peers. Using the EBP process I outlined in this section, I was able to use the I Can Problem Solve (ICPS) program with him in a classroom group to enable Matt and his classmates to use their words effectively. After several months of the classroom group intervention, Matt's behavior had changed to the point where he was volunteering to do role-plays of ICPS situations in front of the class!

ADHD
Step 1: Creating an Answerable Question

Recent prevalence studies estimate that almost 10% of American students are diagnosed with ADHD (Teasley, 2006). Perhaps owing to its prominence in my Illinois survey data, it's clear that despite the explosion in information, diagnoses, and treatments for ADHD, there is still some question about

Table 5.2 School-Based Social Skills Interventions: Results From an EBP Process

INTERVENTION AND INTERVENTION RATING (EFFECTIVE, PROMISING, OR EMERGING)	POPULATION STUDIED	EXPERIMENTAL OR QUASI-EXPERIMENTAL DESIGN?	RANDOM ASSIGNMENT OF SUBJECTS?	STUDY DONE IN A SCHOOL?	RESULTS OF STUDY	SIX-MONTH FOLLOW-UP RESULTS?	MATERIAL AND TRAINING COSTS HOW TO FIND OUT MORE
Effective							
Promoting Alternative Thinking Strategies (PATHS) (Blueprints, 2007)	Elementary-age children	Yes, either experimental or quasi-experimental design	Yes	Yes	Improved self-control, recognition of emotions in themselves and others, increased ability to tolerate frustration	Yes	http://www.channing-bete.com/prevention-programs/paths/ $719 for the K-6 curriculum modules.
Promising							
Go Grrls Program (LeCroy, 2004)	Middle school girls	Yes, random assignment of students to treatment or control	Yes Overall n = 118	Yes	Significant improvement for control group on measures of attitudes toward	No; study did only pre- and posttest measures	Go Grrls Workbook ($11 on amazon.com); additional training (cost not

Program	Population	Design	Control condition		Outcomes	Follow-up	Availability
I Can Problem Solve (ICPS) (Shure & Spivack, 1982)	K-1 and fifth- to sixth-grade inner city children	Yes, quasi-experimental	Unclear; most students were given the ICPS intervention at intervals to act as controls for the other conditions	Yes	Significant decreases in impulsive behaviors and increases in students acting less inhibited in appropriate ways compared to control conditions; same results seen in fifth- to sixth-grade sample, but more sessions (dosage) were needed	Yes	ICPS book ($40, available at www.researchpress.com); Unclear if additional training to lead ICPS groups is needed for teachers and school social workers: additional information available at Shure's Web site, http://www.thinkingchild.com/.

body image, assertiveness, self-efficacy, and self-liking

right after the end of the intervention

specified available at Go Grrrls Web site: http://www.public.asu.edu/~lecroy/gogrrrls/gogrrrls.htm).

(continued)

Table 5.2 Continued

INTERVENTION AND INTERVENTION RATING (EFFECTIVE, PROMISING, OR EMERGING)	POPULATION STUDIED	EXPERIMENTAL OR QUASI-EXPERIMENTAL DESIGN?	RANDOM ASSIGNMENT OF SUBJECTS?	STUDY DONE IN A SCHOOL?	RESULTS OF STUDY	SIX-MONTH FOLLOW-UP RESULTS?	MATERIAL AND TRAINING COSTS HOW TO FIND OUT MORE
Metropolitan Area Child Study (MACS, 2007)	Elementary-age boys and girls in high-risk schools in city and suburban contexts 1991 to 1997	Yes, random assignment of schools and classrooms to treatment or control conditions	Yes Overall $n = 4000$	Yes	Significant decreases in aggressive behavior and increases in academic achievement in comparison to control groups	Yes, follow-ups from 1991 to 1997	Contact information for researchers is readily available and listed below; however, specifics about the actual interventions used, training availability/costs were not easily accessible. Contact Patrick Tolan, University of Illinois-Chicago Institute for Juvenile Research: http://www.psych.uic.edu/fcrg/macs.html

Program	Population	Experimental design			Outcomes	Follow-up	Additional information
Open Circle Program (OCP) (Hennessey, 2007)	Fourth-grade children	Yes, quasi-experimental, with treatment and control classrooms	No	Yes	Teachers rated students in the OCP groups as improving in social skills and decreasing problem behaviors compared to control groups	No, just pre- and posttest measures	Contact information for Open Circle Program http://www.open-circle.org/. Training per teacher $775, $390 for K-5 curriculum guide (one for each grade level).
Reaching Educators, Children and Parents (RECAP) (Han, Catron, Weiss, & Marciel, 2005)	Pre-K children	Yes, schools randomly assigned to RECAP program or comparison group	Yes	Yes	Pre- and posttest measures of child social skills showed significant treatment effects for teacher ratings, not parent ratings	No, just pre- and posttest measures	No cost information available; the article implies that training in the program is needed but no specifics listed. Contact information: Dr. Susan Han, Vanderbilt Institute for Public Policy Studies.

(continued)

Table 5.2 Continued

INTERVENTION AND INTERVENTION RATING (EFFECTIVE, PROMISING, OR EMERGING)	POPULATION STUDIED	EXPERIMENTAL OR QUASI-EXPERIMENTAL DESIGN?	RANDOM ASSIGNMENT OF SUBJECTS?	STUDY DONE IN A SCHOOL?	RESULTS OF STUDY	SIX-MONTH FOLLOW-UP RESULTS?	MATERIAL AND TRAINING COSTS HOW TO FIND OUT MORE
School and Home in Partnership (SHIP)	K-3-grade children	Yes, students and their parents randomly assigned to treatment or control condition	Yes, overall $n = 329$ families	Yes	Significant improvement on only two ratings: parent ratings of their child's antisocial behavior and coercive behavior with peers; teacher ratings and direct observation revealed no significant differences between control and treatment conditions	No, just pre- and posttest measures for Cooke et al. (2007); Grossman et al. (1997) did do a 6-month follow-up and found Second Step gains had maintained at 6 months	Social skill intervention component is based on (1) the CLASS program, which dates from the 1970s and was not easily accessible via web searches; (2) Dina the Dinosaur (for 4 to 8 year olds) Cost for Dina manual and resources $1075 at http://www.incredibleyears.com/index.asp

| Second Step (many authors; most recent study Cooke et al., 2007) | Pre K-8 grade | No, for Cooke et al. study, all students in the district in 3rd to 5th grades received Second Step | No, overall $n = 741$; Several other studies on Second Step consulted for this review had some control groups but were unclear on random assignment | Yes | Significant improvements in positive approach-coping, caring-cooperative behavior, suppression of aggression, and consideration of others, but no changes in aggressive-antisocial behaviors | Second Step curriculum guides $799 K-5, and $535 for sixth to eighth-grade Program Web site: http://www.cfchildren.org/programs/ssp/overview/ |

Emerging

No studies were found in the EBP process search that qualified as "Emerging."

how best to treat this disorder, both in school and community settings. Indeed, some critics of psychiatric treatment for children question whether ADHD is overdiagnosed in kids and whether it even exists at all, given the international disparities between ADHD treatment in the United States and other industrialized and developing nations (Robison, Sclar, Skaer, & Galin, 1999). For the purpose of this section, we will appraise the evidence on how school social workers can treat ADHD effectively, though readers are encouraged to explore alternative views of ADHD and its potential over-identification in American education (for a good introduction and for more information on this controversy, please see the Public Broadcasting Service (PBS) frontline documentary, "Medicating Kids," at http://www.pbs.org/wgbh/pages/frontline/shows/medicating/).

Students who have ADHD have the following symptoms, according to the *DSM-IV TR* (American Psychiatric Association, 2000). Most students are diagnosed with ADHD by an outside medical professional such as a pediatrician or child psychiatrist, though it is possible that school districts can offer special education services based on their educational observations and assessment related to their belief that the student exhibits symptoms of ADHD (Teasley, 2006). Students who have ADHD are at risk for a variety of negative outcomes in childhood and eventually later in life, including poor peer relationships, home and school discipline problems, and academic underachievement (Litner, 2003). At the same time, students with ADHD can also be creative, high-energy learners who keep their peers, parents, and teachers on their toes with their rapid-fire ideas and overall intensity (Nylund, 2000).

For this section, our EBP question is, "What are effective school-based treatments for students with ADHD that work whether or not the student is taking ADHD medication?"

Steps 2 and 3: Investigating and Appraising the Evidence

As Table 5.3 shows, there are a number of promising treatments available for ADHD in schools, based on teaching students self-regulation skills and modifying their classroom setting to promote more on-task and appropriate behavior. Though pharmacological interventions are recognized by many parents and teachers as the main way to treat ADHD in kids (Wolraich, Wibbelsman, & Brown, 2005) many researchers and practitioners are turning to multimodal treatment strategies that incorporate medication, behavioral training at home and school, teacher consultation, and parent training, recognizing that not all students are helped by medication alone and that some families are expressing reservations about putting their children on ADHD stimulant medication (Evans et al., 2006; Teasley, 2006). One positive aspect of the current treatment science on ADHD is that a number of interventions (e.g., parent training, behavior therapy, classroom management strategies, and stimulant medications) have shown moderate to strong impacts on reducing student impulsivity and increasing student achievement and on-task behavior, increasing the range of choices that parents and children have in treating ADHD (DuPaul & Eckert, 1997; DuPaul & Weyandt, 2006; Evans et al., 2006).

Step 4: Adapting and Applying the Evidence

The first step with any student who presents with what looks like behaviors consistent with ADHD is to make sure that a good assessment is completed. Many parents are rightfully skeptical about the immediate discussion of ADHD and medication, particularly when they are new to the school and/or a member of a minority group that has historically been overlabelled for special education services (Watkins & Kurtz, 2001). An EBP process may need to be started just to establish what the parents want to know about ADHD: its prevalence in children of their son's or daughter's age, and the proven effectiveness of non-medication treatment in treating ADHD. Fortunately, if parents are interested in exploring whether their child meets the criteria for ADHD, several reliable and valid instruments exist to help school social workers begin to help parents and school colleagues to figure out whether the student may have ADHD (a list of good ADHD assessment are available in Teasley, 2006).

Second, many parents, after learning that their child has symptoms indicative of ADHD, may wish to pursue additional medical, psychological, and educational services to assist their child. This is again where an EBP process can be invaluable, as so many parents over the years have told me how confused and worn out they feel trying to manage their child's new diagnosis and filter and interpret all the claims they hear about effective ADHD treatments. Table 5.3 can be a good starting point for work with parents, as many of the promising and emerging interventions listed there may be the ones that parents and children are willing to pursue, especially when they learn from you that the interventions themselves have been rigorously evaluated by independent researchers. It will also be helpful for school social workers to bring their own practice experience to the evidence in Table 5.3, as some of the interventions there may be the ones they have employed in the past.

Table 5.3 School-Based Attention-Deficit Disorder Interventions: Results From an EBP Process

INTERVENTION RATING	POPULATION STUDIED	EXPERIMENTAL OR QUASI-EXPERIMENTAL DESIGN?	RANDOM ASSIGNMENT OF SUBJECTS?	STUDY CONDUCTED IN A SCHOOL SETTING?	RESULTS OF STUDY	SIX-MONTH FOLLOW-UP RESULTS	MATERIAL AND TRAINING COSTS HOW TO FIND OUT MORE
Effective							
Based on the criteria, there were no studies that were evaluated as "Effective."							
Promising							
Behavioral Management Interventions (DuPaul & Eckert, 1997)	Meta-analysis of 63 ADHD school-based intervention studies from 1971 to 1995 (for another smaller meta-analysis, see Reid, Trout, & Schartz, 2005)	Qualified Yes; some of the studies were single-subject designs, but most were quasi-experimental	Unclear	Yes (one of the criteria for including in the meta-analysis)	Studies with a control group had a moderate (.45) effect size for helping students manage their behavior through a variety of behavior-based intervention strategies	n/a	All the studies used for the meta-analysis are clearly listed in the article's references.

| Challenging Horizons Program (CHP) (Evans et al., 2005) | Middle school students n = 7 | No | No | Yes (on school grounds after school) | Based on multiple measures of single-subject designs, most students demonstrated moderate gains in both academic and social functioning | No (authors are still analyzing initial data and plan further follow-up) | No information on cost of materials and training possibilities; Program has a Web site that describes its program in more detail: http://chp.cisat.jmu.edu/chp.html. |
| Modifying Classroom Environment and Instructional Strategies (Zentall, 2005) | Students in K-12 settings; this is a review of ADHD school intervention strategies | No | No | Yes | No method is specified for how studies were selected or evaluated; still, the studies cited do indicate that making the classroom environment more | No | No training or materials are listed in the article. |

(continued)

Table 5.3 Continued

INTERVENTION RATING	POPULATION STUDIED	EXPERIMENTAL OR QUASI-EXPERIMENTAL DESIGN?	RANDOM ASSIGNMENT OF SUBJECTS?	STUDY CONDUCTED IN A SCHOOL SETTING?	RESULTS OF STUDY	SIX-MONTH FOLLOW-UP RESULTS	MATERIAL AND TRAINING COSTS HOW TO FIND OUT MORE
					stimulating and sensory-rich can help students with ADHD maintain their attention more successfully		
Emerging Note-taking skills (Direct Note-taking Activity or DNA) (Evans et al., 1994–1995, 2005)	Adolescents in a summer day program for teens with ADHD	No, pre- and post-test design only	No	No (conducted in a summer day program for high school youth)	Students learned the strategies and had better attention and less disruptive behavior during lessons.	No	No training information; cite of article can be found at (Evans et al., 1995)

| Teaching Self-Monitoring of Academic Performance and Behavior (Harris et al., 1994, 2005) | Third to fifth graders $n = 6$ | No | No | Yes | Self-monitoring of attention by students increased spelling study behaviors more than monitoring performance | No | No training information. |

The combination of practice wisdom, client preferences, and solid empirical testing of the interventions being offered to clients may prove to be the combination that makes the intervention ultimately successful.

Step 5: Evaluating the Results of an EBP Process

Carl didn't want anyone to know he had ADHD. A very proud sixth-grade boy, he had told his parents that he was tired of taking medication too and that he was going to solve his ADHD "on his own." I was seeing him weekly as part of his individualized education plan (IEP), and his parents called me concerned that without his medication, Carl wouldn't pass his classes. I developed a plan with Carl that we would try some of the classroom behavior ideas outlined in DuPaul and Eckert's (1997) meta-analysis. He agreed to try the ideas as long as I promised that if he showed he could handle his schoolwork this way, I would support his desire to try being off ADHD medication for a while. We worked out a behavior plan that involved Carl self-regulating his behavior via a checklist on his desk, and then comparing his results with his teacher's observations. With the feedback and support of his teacher, Carl began to see that he could handle his schoolwork and pay attention more than he had before, and he was so pleased by this change that he told his parents that he would continue taking the medication "for them," just not at school.

Student Anxiety
Step 1: Creating an Answerable Question

Anxiety disorders affect roughly 13 out of 100 young people, affecting girls more than boys (SAMHSA, 2007). While this section will focus on generalized anxiety disorder (GAD) and ways to treat it in a school setting, there are a number of other anxiety disorders in childhood that present in school settings, including panic attacks, separation anxiety disorder, and phobias (Camacho & Hunter, 2006). The characteristics of these other anxiety disorders as well as GAD include worrying excessively about everyday events, refusing to go to school, and having difficulty concentrating, somatic complaints, and sleep disturbances (American Psychiatric Association, 2000). Students who have untreated anxiety disorders are at risk for school underachievement, poor social relationships, and eventual substance abuse as they turn to efforts to self-medicate and cope with their anxiety (Masia-Warner et al., 2005).

For this section, I chose to pose this EBP question, "What are effective school-based interventions to help students manage their symptoms of anxiety?"

Steps 2 and 3: Investigating and Appraising the Evidence

Table 5.4 indicates that there are several effective and emerging interventions that school social workers can begin using immediately to help students with anxiety symptoms. This is in addition to the growing use of selective serotonin reuptake inhibitors (SSRIs) and other psychiatric medications that are being used to treat anxiety in children (Anxiety Disorders Association of America [ADAA], 2007), though there is still some concern for some parents because the FDA hasn't formally approved their use for children (Bentley & Collins, 2006). The best thing about much of the research on anxiety treatments, based on the EBP search conducted for this chapter, was the relatively large number of well-controlled studies that had been completed in school settings. Though there are a host of complicating issues (students who have comorbid disorders such as ADHD or depression, or who also have learning problems), anxiety is one area of school-based mental health that might be implemented fairly quickly and affordably for a broad range of ages and population groups in American schools (Oswald & Mazefsky, 2006).

Step 4: Adapting and Applying the Evidence

Just as with ADHD, it is important that school social workers work closely with the client system (including the student's health care providers) to help establish that the diagnosis of anxiety is a correct and solid one. There are a number of clinical interview scaled instruments to help school social workers identify whether a student is suffering from anxiety (for a recent summary of good anxiety assessment scales, see Balon, 2007; Camacho & Hunter, 2006). In addition to offering these scales to students and their parents, it is important for school social workers to develop linkages with child psychiatrists and pediatric neurologists that might be able to help with the diagnostic work necessary to establish that the student has an anxiety disorder. Additionally, because the vast majority of students are unlikely to get outside psychological counseling treatment for their anxiety disorders (Essau, Conradt, & Petterman, 1999), the more that school social workers can provide to students at school, the more potential benefit that the interventions noted in Table 5.4 might have for students.

Step 5: Evaluating the Results

Sally wanted to stop sweating in school. She worried constantly about her work, her friends, her family, and her future. She was a capable and hardworking seventh grader, but she couldn't see herself that way, especially

Table 5.4 School-Based Anxiety Interventions: Results From an EBP Process

INTERVENTION AND INTERVENTION RATING (EFFECTIVE, PROMISING, OR EMERGING)	POPULATION STUDIED	EXPERIMENTAL OR QUASI-EXPERIMENTAL DESIGN?	RANDOM ASSIGNMENT OF SUBJECTS?	STUDY CONDUCTED IN A SCHOOL SETTING?	RESULTS OF STUDY	SIX-MONTH FOLLOW-UP RESULTS?	MATERIAL AND TRAINING COSTS HOW TO FIND OUT MORE
Effective							
Coping Cat (Kendall, 1994; Kendall et al., 1997)	Children aged 8 to 13	Yes, random assignment of students to treatment or wait-list control group; first study n = 47, second study n = 94	Yes	Yes, though initial studies were done in a clinic setting	Based on pre- and posttests and self and parent reports, students showed improvement on their coping skills and decreased anxiety level	Yes, both initial studies showed gains were maintained at one year	Coping Cat Workbook by Kendall & Hedtke (2006), $27 at amazon.com; a DVD of the Coping Cat for use with students is available for $56 at www.workbookpublishing.com; No cost information on training for the Coping Cat Program.

Program	Population	Design		Results	Follow-up	Availability/Cost
FRIENDS (Lowry-Webster, Barrett, & Lock, 2003)	Children aged 6 to 16	Schools randomly assigned to FRIENDS or no-treatment control; $n = 594$	Yes	Yes	Students in the FRIENDS group reported fewer anxiety symptoms at posttest	Yes, gains maintained at 1-year follow-up	Program is based out of Australia at http://www.friendsinfo.net/Cost of initial packet containing manual and materials $150; Web site is unclear about whether trainings are available outside of Australia

Promising

Cool Kids Program (Mifsud & Rapee, 2005)	Children aged 9 to 10, from low-income schools in the Australia	Yes, schools randomly assigned to treatment or control	Yes	Yes	Symptoms of anxiety decreased in treatment group compared to control	No, researchers only did follow-up at 4 months (though they claim the students had maintained their gains)	Cool Kids manuals available for $75 for child/adolescent levels at the researcher's Web site: http://www.psy.mq.edu.au/MUARU/books/prof.htm Training is encouraged, though training appears to only be offered in Australia at present.

Emerging

No studies were found in the EBP process search that qualified as "Emerging."

when her anxious thoughts intruded. I worked with her using some of the cognitive techniques from the Coping Cat intervention (Kendall, 1994), and after several months, she was able to successfully combat her anxious thoughts at school. Interestingly, with some initial success from my work with her, she then told her parents that she was interested in seeing a therapist that summer to keep working on her "worries."

Using the EBP Process for Student Mental Health Problems: Final Thoughts

These examples of the EBP process, while likely to figure in the work of most school social workers, are hardly an exhaustive list. There are many more mental health and behavioral issues present in school settings that I didn't have the space to cover here. The beauty of the EBP process is that it allows school social workers to apply EBP to nearly any clinical issue that comes through their office door, and while there is certainly no guarantee that school social workers will find good evidence on the problem they investigate, the process still can be conducted for nearly any issue school social workers face.

I know this because, for the past 10 years, I have been using elements of the EBP process to enhance my school social work practice. Using the EBP process to understand and evaluate evidence gets easier each time I do it, but there are still challenges to doing EBP in schools that are real and deserve mentioning. Time will always be a consideration, as many of the interventions school social workers apply are grounded in short-term crisis intervention conditions. Access to good research information will be a persistent issue as well, with both computer access and/or access to many leading research databases, like the Academic Premier/EBSCOHost journal database I used for this chapter, not always guaranteed. School social workers I supervise and consult with often tell me that they don't feel that their schools give them continuing education and professional development that is relevant to their needs as school social workers. Here is a great opportunity for school social workers to advocate for their district to purchase database subscriptions and give them additional training in the EBP process. I know that I would have loved to get trained in these ideas and methods rather than sitting through technology workshops touting the latest reading software or seminars on improving math instruction.

6

■ ■ ■

EBP, Special Education, and Response to Intervention (RTI): How RTI Could Reshape School Social Work Practice to Become (Hopefully) More Effective and Evidence Based

For this chapter, I will briefly review the Individuals with Disabilities Education Improvement Act (IDEA) reauthorization of 2004 that added RTI to the range of services and that supports school districts in developing innovative programs to address student academic and social/emotional problems prior to providing special education services. The 3-tier process of RTI (and its implications for school social work practice), as well as a brief appraisal of the current evidence on RTI's effectiveness in schools, will be discussed here.

RTI Is a Major Movement in Educational Service Provision

For at-risk students, RTI gained increased prominence and legitimacy when it was included in the 2004 IDEA reauthorization. Now, all public schools have the option to institute RTI programs to aid students prior to referring them for special education evaluation and services (Barnett, Daly, Jones, & Lentz, 2004). The RTI process represents a significant opportunity for school social workers to join other school professionals in designing interventions that are based on empirical evidence (both from the research literature and from the students' own performance history) and are regularly evaluated for how effectively they are addressing the students' learning problems. In addition to describing how RTI has been implemented by school social workers, this chapter will offer ideas for school social workers to evaluate RTI, both as a process to infuse a "data-driven" approach to education and as a process that risks overriding individual student, family, and cultural contextual factors unless it is done with the same ethical commitments that this book argues are part of the EBP process.

The second concept to be discussed is the special education services under IDEA. This special education law is now in its 30th year and has had a major impact on schools in general and school social work services in particular. A related concept to IDEA to be defined will be the individualized education plan (IEP), the legal documenting process that schools use to assess students and deliver special education service. Finally, the specific applications of IDEA and IEP services for school social work will be explored.

Special Education: A Brief History of IDEA

Special education is an aspect of American education that covers a wide range of students with a wide range of disabilities. Presently, there are fourteen different categories of student disability, running the gamut from severe mental and physical impairments to autistic spectrum disorders to behavior disorders (Altshuler & Kopels, 2003). The IDEA was first passed in the mid-1970s, and the growth in the country's special education student population has been dramatic in the 30 years since IDEA was first passed. In 1976 there were 3.7 million students found eligible by student service diagnostic teams for special education services; in 1999 to 2000, this number had gone up by 65% to 6.1 million students (Horn & Tynan, 2001).

Special education advocates might respond to these statistics by saying that IDEA has only gotten better at identifying students at risk and at doing the hard work of assessing their eligibility for special education services based on rigorous criteria. However, Ysseldyke (2001) and other prominent critics of special education criteria assert that because there are no universally accepted and diagnostic criteria for what constitutes many special education categories, there is no way to empirically test whether our methods have gotten better, or whether we're just finding more students eligible. The learning disability (LD) category is instructive here. LD is by far the largest category of special education eligibility, with over 50% of students receiving special education in 2000 having an LD label (Pascopella, 2003). However, some scholars argue that the lack of clear diagnostic criteria for LD across all schools makes it possible that "over 80 percent of all schoolchildren in the U.S. could qualify as having a learning disability under one (state) definition or another" (Horn & Tynan, 2001). All of these statistics also reflect both a racial and a gender gap in special education placement that appears to cut across all racial groups: Girls are less likely to be screened for and placed in self-contained special education environments, particularly for LD and emotional disability (ED) issues (Watkins & Kurtz, 2001), whereas African American and Latino boys are overrepresented in special education placements (Losen & Orfield, 2002; Smith, 2004; United States House Committee on Education and the Workforce, 2001).

Proponents of special education argue that special education is there to help those who need it. And if black boys (and other boys of all colors, who are all overrepresented in special education compared to girls of all races) are having trouble learning, shouldn't we try to help them? The answer is yes and no. IDEA, as it was originally conceived in 1975, was to enable mentally and physically disabled students to go to school in their home district. Thirty years later, IDEA has accomplished this worthy goal, but has also created two other categories (the range of disorders that fall under LD and the emotional/behavioral labels of ED) that have far outgrown their original mandates (Horn & Tynan, 2001; Watkins & Kurtz, 2001).

Special Education and RTI

Though referrals for special education testing appear to be growing nationally, there still is a fierce debate in the research literature about whether the majority of these special education students with LD and ED labels are "better off" than they would have been if they had no special education services and instead had other more targeted academic and/or behavioral interventions without the special education label (Heward, 2003; Horn & Tynan, 2001). The Presidential Commission on Excellence in Special Education recognized these issues directly, and recommended that schools adopt more pre-referral programs such as RTI to help serve students without using the route of special education referral, diagnosis, and referral (President's Commission on Excellence in Special Education 2002).

Advocates, policy makers, and scholars have all stepped into the debate over "what works" in special education to ask: Can the process of identifying, testing, and labeling be made more effective? And before students are even found eligible for special education services, can behavioral and academic interventions be put in place to help them succeed? And if this is possible, what are the most effective "pre-referral interventions" that have been empirically validated?

Scholars believe that the current process of identifying and "treating" at-risk students, being based largely on the discrepancy model involving IQ tests to determine eligibility and behavior modification programs to manage disruptive student behavior, is badly in need of revision and enhancement (Presidential New Freedom Commission, 2002). Many scholars, particularly those working in the fields of education, school psychology, and school social work, advocate more collaborative approaches, including interventions based on components derived from the diverse fields of applied behavior analysis, solution-focused therapy and the strengths perspective (Brown-Chidsey & Steege, 2005; Fuchs, Mock, Morgan, & Young, 2003; Watkins & Kurtz, 2001). The evidence is growing that interventions by school social workers who focus on designing interventions rooted in student strengths can improve social, behavioral, and academic outcomes for at-risk students (Corcoran, 1998; Franklin, 2005; Newsome, 2004; Watkins & Kurtz, 2001).

Additionally, school social workers are increasingly being required by their districts to provide behavior management consultations to their schools via the functional analysis component of the IEP process, often called functional behavioral assessments (FBAs) for functional behavior analysis (Illinois Association of School Social Workers [IASSW], 2005). Initial studies of FBAs involving school-based mental health professionals show that these analyses and the resultant behavior intervention plans (BIPs) can be effective in modifying student behaviors and assisting teachers in managing their classroom, though a recent review raises concerns about the need for behavior interventions to "be matched to the severity of the behavior problem exhibited by the individual" (Gresham, 2004, p. 337). This is a concern for the field, as researchers are careful to encourage researchers and practitioners to avoid overstating the impact of behavioral interventions in schools without paying sufficient attention to doing the work of observing actual student behavior and designing appropriate supports to modify their responses to their school environment. Van Acker and his colleagues (2005) found that a majority of IEPs written for students with behavior problems did not have sufficient empirical foundations to be effective in helping students with behavior problems. The researchers also found that the current state of functional analyses of behavior in schools was so poor that most IEPs would not be sturdy enough to withstand legal challenges from parents (Van Acker, Boreson, Gable, & Potterton, 2005). Are school social workers adequately prepared with the skills and knowledge to do effective functional analyses of student behavior? Limited evidence is available to answer this question: In my Illinois survey, 53% said they had some training in designing and implementing behavioral interventions, but only 15% identified that training as "very good" (Kelly, manuscript under review). There is a significant need for more research in this area, particularly in how best to help train professionals in implementing behavioral interventions in their school contexts that have shown promising results in other school contexts.

What We Can Do: New/Old Roles for School Social Workers in the RTI Process

At our Family and Schools Partnership Program, I was consulting with a colleague who had just been hired in a local suburban Chicago school district. She was excited to have found the position and was excited to be working with a K-6 population. She told me that her major concern was that she wasn't sure the principal understood what school social workers do. "They want me to help case manage their early intervention program for under-performing readers, and I told them I don't have any training in reading, and they said, 'we want you to make sure the services are in place and going well.' What do they think I'm going to do? Aren't I supposed to take care of the counseling needs of these children, and leave the reading instruction to the reading specialists?"

To this point in this chapter, I've focused on special education and RTI as being largely based on helping remove behavioral barriers to learning, which is understandable given the traditional role that school social workers have fulfilled in the special education process. However, a crucial aspect of RTI is one that might seem extraneous to most school social workers' role in schools: the importance of helping kids in early grades learn to read. This is clearly the focus of RTI nationally, that is, the focus on using the Dynamic Indicators of Basic Early Literacy Skills (DIBELS) to assess whole-school and individual student progress in reading in early grades (DIBELS, 2007). Literacy researchers and RTI advocates have teamed up to argue that early reading intervention can be instrumental in preventing future negative learning outcomes for students, as well as possibly diverting some students from special education services (Presidential Commission, 2002). The reauthorization of IDEA in 2004 recognized the potential of RTI programs as a way to address learning problems for students, giving districts the option to use up to 15% of their funds to implement RTI-based programs in their schools (IDEA, 2004).

Given that many school social workers are already involved in the special education referral, diagnosis, and treatment process, it makes sense to think about how school social workers might become part of the RTI process as well. In some schools, the student support team charged with conducting RTI evaluations and delivering services will likely involve the same personnel as the special education diagnostic team. Additionally, because RTI is meant to target students quickly and measure impacts of interventions in a systematic and ongoing fashion, the entire process is more intensive than a standard special education referral and requires additional engagement with students and families to make sure that they understand the process fully and are committed to making it work. Finally, a major area of RTI that has been under-researched to this point is how the RTI model can be used to facilitate the implementation of behavioral interventions for students who might otherwise be referred directly to a special education team for possible behavior disorder/emotional disturbance services (Gresham, 2004). I believe that in all of these areas (i.e., case management, parent engagement, group facilitation, and behavioral interventions) school social workers have a plethora of skills that can make them important contributors to RTI programs in their schools.

School Social Workers as Case Managers

In these early stages of RTI implementation nationwide, many schools and stakeholders will have questions about what the benefits and costs of RTI are for them. One common critique offered for initial RTI efforts is that it can be time and cost prohibitive because teachers are required to spend a lot of time documenting their students' performance and meeting in teams to collaborate on strategies to increase student performance (Fasko, 2006). Given all the time involved, it is easy to imagine these interventions becoming fragmented and hard to track, as normal school life takes over and the constant ups and downs of classrooms take precedence. School social workers, with our profession's long tradition of case management, are uniquely positioned to offer assistance to the RTI process, helping teachers, students, parents, and other RTI team members stay focused on the targets of the RTI process. Research on how school social workers can help case managers in the RTI process is needed because it is clear from my anecdotal experience in Illinois that several school social workers can (and do) make a difference when they help to case manage RTI programmatic interventions.

School Social Workers Can Help Increase Parent Involvement in the RTI Process

Since the beginning of the profession, school social workers have been instrumental in linking schools to families and back again (Franklin & Gerlach, 2006; Shaffer 2007). This area of family engagement is crucial in RTI because researchers cite the struggle of linking the largely school-based interventions associated with RTI to what parents can do to build on these gains at home. School social workers are often already poised to do the parent engagement role in RTI: They know their school's families and are often the persons in the school that parents turn to for consultation and crisis intervention (Constable, 2006). For this reason, as well as the others I discuss in this section, it seems advisable for school social workers to advocate for their involvement on RTI teams, even the ones that are explicitly focused on literacy skills only.

School Social Workers as RTI Group Facilitators

In addition to case management and family engagement skills, school social workers have expertise in group process that is vital to the RTI process. The nature of RTI involves the identification of specific areas to treat, usually in relation to reading difficulties. Despite the increasing number of standardized reading instruments, there is still the human factor that needs attention, as RTI strives to involve the student, the student's family, and the students' teachers in an intensive process of discovery and (hopefully) successful interventions. Because RTI is in part designed to address the overrepresentation of certain groups in special education and intervene more quickly with those groups, there is a need for all members of the student's support system to be on board as the interventions proceed (Fasko, 2006). In several schools I've consulted at, school social workers have easily stepped into the role of RTI team facilitators, using their listening and conflict resolution skills to help RTI teams focus their work and stay on track. Empirical study of potential school social work effectiveness as RTI team leaders (particularly in the areas of case management and parent engagement) would be a worthwhile contribution to the practice and research literature in schools.

School Social Workers as Part of an RTI Process Focused on Student Behavior

A recent review of school-based behavioral interventions (Gresham, 2004) outlined the potential benefits and challenges of applying an RTI approach to helping students who have emotional and behavioral problems that present in school settings. One potential benefit from RTI for behavior problems could involve helping students manage their behavior in ways that might assist them avoid disciplinary action and/or referral for special education evaluation because of their behavioral difficulties (Reschly, 2004). Second, because minorities are overrepresented in the high-incidence special education category of emotional disturbance/behavior disorder, an

RTI process that addresses student behavior problems early and without special education services might prove attractive to school districts and parents concerned about possible minority overrepresentation in their special education programs. RTI could also be integrated into a larger program of positive behavioral supports (PBSs) to help the whole school engage in more pro-social behavior and decrease discipline problems (for more information on examples of PBS interventions, please see Chapter 7 in this book).

However, there are numerous challenges to implementing RTI for students with behavior problems, and school social workers need to think about these issues as they and their RTI teams consider how to help students. Many students will present with a mixture of behavioral and academic concerns, and it can be hard to untangle how best to proceed, particularly when many RTI teams may be more oriented to treating reading difficulties and feel less skilled in addressing behavior problems (Gresham, 2004). Schools may see students with behavior problems as more "radioactive," and requiring more serious intervention that involves a special education case study. The case study process, though slower in some ways and prone to the aforementioned concern about minority overrepresentation, does give schools the option of pursuing a self-contained classroom placement or even an out-of-district placement, which the school can argue for as a way to both serve the student's behavioral needs and also keep the home school safe. However, as Van Acker et al. (2005) showed in their review of FBAs, many current behavior analyses in schools lack basic empirical data and are often hard to understand, let alone implement and monitor as closely as the RTI process calls for. Finally, the RTI process itself may be revealed by further study to be better suited to problems that can be more clearly benchmarked, normed, and measured than many emotional/behavioral problems (Gresham, 2004; Walker, 2004).

On the basis of a review of current education/behavioral databases in August 2007, it isn't clear how many schools are using RTI to address the needs of students with behavior problems as well as the needs of students with reading difficulties. It's possible that with further study on its potential utility and effectiveness, schools might adopt the RTI model as a general pre-referral intervention to help them document their interventions before referring students on to a special education evaluation, as some national organizations have suggested. Whatever the future holds for RTI as a behavioral intervention, the need for school social workers to join other professionals in designing and implementing behavior plans is only likely to increase in years to come.

7

■ ■ ■

Helping Families and School Communities: EBP in Action

Families and Schools in Crisis: Using the EBP Process to Address Family Issue and Whole-School Problems Many School Social Workers Encounter

This chapter will identify issues and solutions to problems that families and whole-school communities experience. Drawing from my Illinois survey data, I share two major family stressors that school social workers say their families struggle with (i.e., divorce and poverty) and show how an EBP process can help school social workers find the best available evidence to understand and intervene with those family stressors. Finally, this chapter will share two extended case examples of whole-school interventions (quadrant A and D) that made a significant impact on the school community after I used an EBP process to help me assess my school community and intervene effectively.

Divorce and poverty were cited as major family stressors impacting the caseload of over 60% of the school social workers in Illinois. These significant family stressors are themselves useful areas for an EBP approach because they highlight how complex and multifaceted family-based work in a school becomes when practitioners try to work with students dealing with severe or chronic family stress. Summaries of the best available evidence on these family stressors and evidence on effective school and family-based interventions to address these issues will be included in this chapter, along with case examples that show how a school social worker might use an

EBP approach to connect with families dealing with these significant issues. Both treatments rooted in the EBP process described in this book, as well as more manualized treatments that have empirical support, will be described in this chapter to show the diversity of current intervention "evidence" and how it can be appraised and then implemented by school social workers.

Table 7.1 describes the most prominent psychosocial stressors that my Illinois sample respondents said their schools' families face. These intense family stressors make the case not only for additional community-school collaboration to increase family support (particularly in areas of family financial hardship), but also for family-based treatment in schools (divorce/ separation of parents). Using the same basic EBP process approach I outlined in Chapter 5, I will show you how I found out information about these psychosocial stressors, and in one case (divorce/separation of parents) used the EBP research I obtained to design an intervention for students at my school. I will close this chapter with some further comments on ways to effectively search for information on family-based stressors and apply that information to your particular school context.

Table 7.1 Most Prevalent Psychosocial Stressors Affecting Students' Families

	RURAL (%)	URBAN (%)	SUBURBAN (%)	TOTAL (%)
Divorce/separation of parents	82	76.3	88.2	84
Financial hardship	74.1	84.2	64.5	69
Substance abuse in the family	56.8	61.6	44.9	54
Mental illness in another family member (not the student)	51.1	41.2	44.2	45
Domestic violence in the home	32.4	49.2	30.8	36

Note. All figures are percentages and based on data collected from 821 participants who completed the School Social Work Survey. Percentages do not add up to 100%, as respondents could select more than one choice for each question.

Divorce/Separation of Parents

Steps 1, 2 and 3: Creating an Answerable Question and Investigating and Appraising the Evidence

For this EBP process, I posed the question (step 1 of the EBP process) "What are the effective school-based programs that can help children and families deal with the impacts of divorce and separation?" For this EBP process, I consulted the Academic Premier/EBSCO Host database, a well-known social science database that contains full-text articles for over 4500 journals in the social sciences. I searched for the years 2001 to 2007 and used the following search terms: "divorce and children and prevention," "divorce and schools and prevention," "divorce and children and interventions," and "divorce and schools and interventions." I found 23 articles that appeared to address intervention programs for children and families in a school context and read the abstracts for each one, winnowing the articles that dealt directly with school-based interventions and summarizing my findings, as shown in Table 7.2 (steps 2 and 3 of the EBP process). I also consulted some school social work textbooks to help me identify potential effective, promising, and emerging interventions, which are summarized in Table 7.2.

An average of 1.5 million children experience their parents' divorce in the United States each year (Haine, Sandler, Wolchik, Tein, & Dawson-McClure, 2003; National Marriage Project, 2006). Given that 45% of American marriages end in divorce each year, and that these statistics don't count the students who live with single parents who never married, there are clearly many students in schools who are at risk for various negative life outcomes because they are living in single-parent or what social scientists call "fragile" family situations. (The phenomenon of single-parent families and the impact that it has on students' mental health and academic achievement might merit an EBP process all its own for students you may be concerned about.) Divorce affects all races and social classes in the United States, but it hits racial minorities harder, with over 52% of African American children being raised by a single parent, compared to 18% of white children (National Marriage Project, 2006).

Step 4: Applying and Adapting the Evidence

Part of why I thought it would be useful to pose my Client-Oriented Practical Evidence Search (COPES) question the way I did is that in my experience as a school social worker, I have seen a number of students adversely affected by their parents' divorce. Kids I worked with were susceptible to depression,

Table 7.2 Interventions for Children Dealing with Parental Divorce: Results From an EBP Process

INTERVENTION AND INTERVENTION RATING	POPULATION STUDIED	EXPERIMENTAL OR QUASI-EXPERIMENTAL DESIGN?	RANDOM ASSIGNMENT OF SUBJECTS?	STUDY CONDUCTED IN A SCHOOL SETTING?	RESULTS OF STUDY	SIX-MONTH FOLLOW-UP RESULTS
Effective						
Children's Support Group (Stolberg & Mahler, 1994)	Children; 8 to 12 years	Yes, experimental	Yes	Yes	Reduction in both externalizing and internalizing behaviors associated with divorce as well as total DSM-IV clinical profile	Yes, gains were maintained at 1-year follow-up
Children of Divorce Intervention Project (Pedro-Carroll, Sutton, & Wyman, 1999)	K-8 graders	Yes, quasi-experimental	Yes	Yes	Reduction in internalizing and externalizing behaviors and increases in overall coping skills	Yes, gains were maintained at 2-year follow-up

Promising

No studies in this EBP process were found to be "promising."

Emerging

School-based children's divorce groups (Crespi, Gustafson, & Borges, 2005; DeLucia-Waack & Gerrity, 2001; Rich, Molloy, Hart, Ginsberg, & Mulvey, 2007)	K-12 students	No; for each of the three articles the authors offer a model of how they conduct divorce groups in schools for children	No	Yes	No outcome data is shared in these articles beyond case studies and the authors' reflections on the process of leading the groups	No
Individual therapy for children of divorce (McConnell & Sim, 2000)	Wide range of ages, average age 11 years ($n = 24$); mothers were also included in the treatment as indicated by specific needs of the counseling	No, authors used semistructured qualitative interviews with children and mothers pre- and posttreatment	No	No	Roughly half the mothers and children said they benefited from the counseling; no specific variables of child and child/mother functioning were included in the study	No

anxiety, difficulty forming good peer relationships, and poor academic achievement as they struggled to cope with their loss and the disruption divorce had caused in their lives. Longitudinal research shows that between 20% and 25% of students exhibit serious mental health problems related to their parents' divorce (Sharlene et al., 2002), and some studies claim that the risk of adult mental health problems can be increased by as much as 40% (National Marriage Project, 2006). Although there is still controversy about how much of a long-term negative impact divorce has on children (for a good review, see Amato, 2000), clearly school social workers in my sample saw it as a major stressor that they felt they needed to address with their students and families.

The EBP process detailed here revealed two "effective" interventions that I might work on immediately adopting in my school. This is fairly typical in the EBP searches I've done on school-based issues presented by families. (Another example of how much more quadrant A and B research we need!) What I was able to gain information on was at least two well-supported interventions that could possibly be adapted to a school context. In each of the interventions I found, the researchers had provided contact information and further resources to consult, and I have included them in Table 7.2.

Financial Hardship/Poverty

Steps 1, 2 and 3: Creating an Answerable Question and Investigating and Appraising the Evidence

For the family stressor financial hardship and poverty, I chose to ask a risk question drawn from Gibbs (2003): "What are the risks for children's academic achievement for children living in poverty?" (step 1 of the EBP process). I did an EBSCO search for "poverty and risks and schools" and got 14 hits, none of which directly addressed a school social worker's involvement with families in poverty (step 2 of the EBP process). This isn't surprising because I didn't tailor the question to direct interventions this time, unlike previous EBP questions I've shown in this book. I will summarize one particularly interesting finding I discovered in Box 7.1, concluding with some further ideas on how to use risk EBP questions to help inform interventions in all the clinical quadrants.

Family poverty is increasing in the United States, with 18% of children living in poverty as of 2007 (Center for American Progress, 2007). The adverse impacts of poverty on children's academic preparation and development are serious and potentially long lasting, according to the research I found in my EBP search. For example, 17% of American children live in

BOX 7.1 Twelve Key Steps to Cut Poverty in Half

1. Raise and index the minimum wage to half the average hourly wage. At $5.15, the federal minimum wage is at its lowest level in real terms since 1956. The federal minimum wage was once 50% of the average wage but is now 30% of that wage. Congress should restore the minimum wage to 50% of the average wage, about $8.40 an hour in 2006. Doing so would help nearly 5 million poor workers and nearly 10 million other low-income workers.

2. Expand the Earned Income Tax Credit (EITC) and Child Tax Credit. As an earnings supplement for low-income working families, the EITC raises incomes and helps families build assets. The Child Tax Credit provides a tax credit of up to $1000 per child, but provides no help to the poorest families. We recommend tripling the EITC for childless workers and expanding help to larger working families. We recommend making the Child Tax Credit available to all low- and moderate-income families. Doing so would move as many as 5 million people out of poverty.

3. Promote unionization by enacting the Employee Free Choice Act. The Employee Free Choice Act would require employers to recognize a union after a majority of workers sign cards authorizing union representation and establish stronger penalties for violation of employee rights. The increased union representation made possible by the act would lead to better jobs and less poverty for American workers.

4. Guarantee child care assistance to low-income families and promote early education for all. We propose that the federal and state governments guarantee childcare help to families with incomes below about $40,000 a year, with expanded tax help to higher-earning families. At the same time, states should be encouraged to improve the quality of early education and broaden access for all children. Our childcare expansion would raise employment among low-income parents and help nearly 3 million parents and children escape poverty.

(continued)

5. Create 2 million new "opportunity" housing vouchers and promote equitable development in and around central cities. Nearly 8 million Americans live in neighborhoods of concentrated poverty where at least 40% of residents are poor. Our nation should seek to end concentrated poverty and economic segregation, and promote regional equity and inner-city revitalization. We propose that over the next 10 years the federal government should fund 2 million new "opportunity vouchers" designed to help people live in opportunity-rich areas. Any new affordable housing should be in communities with employment opportunities and high-quality public services, or in gentrifying communities. These housing policies should be part of a broader effort to pursue equitable development strategies in regional and local planning efforts, including efforts to improve schools, create affordable housing, assure physical security, and enhance neighborhood amenities.

6. Connect disadvantaged and disconnected youth with school and work. About 1.7 million poor youth aged 16 to 24 were out of school and out of work in 2005. We recommend that the federal government restore Youth Opportunity Grants to help the most disadvantaged communities and expand funding for effective and promising youth programs—with the goal of reaching 600,000 poor disadvantaged youth through these efforts. We propose a new Upward Pathway program to offer low-income youth opportunities to participate in service and training in fields that are in high demand and provide needed public services.

7. Simplify and expand Pell Grants and make higher education accessible to residents of each state. Low-income youth are much less likely to attend college than their higher income peers, even among those of comparable abilities. Pell Grants play a crucial role for lower-income students. We propose to simplify the Pell Grant application process, gradually raise Pell Grants to reach 70% of the average costs of attending a 4-year public institution, and encourage institutions to do more to raise student completion rates. As the federal government does its part, states should develop strategies to make postsecondary education affordable for all residents, following promising models already underway in a number of states.

(continued)

8. **Help former prisoners find stable employment and reintegrate into their communities.** The United States has the highest incarceration rate in the world. We urge all states to develop comprehensive reentry services aimed at reintegrating former prisoners into their communities with full-time, consistent employment.

9. **Ensure equity for low-wage workers in the Unemployment Insurance system.** Only about 35% of the unemployed, and a smaller share of unemployed low-wage workers, receive unemployment insurance benefits. We recommend that states (with federal help) reform "monetary eligibility" rules that screen out low-wage workers, broaden eligibility for part-time workers and workers who have lost employment as a result of compelling family circumstances, and allow unemployed workers to use periods of unemployment as a time to upgrade their skills and qualifications.

10. **Modernize means-tested benefits programs to develop a coordinated system that helps workers and families.** A well-functioning safety net should help people get into or return to work and ensure a decent level of living for those who cannot work or are temporarily between jobs. Our current system fails to do so. We recommend that governments at all levels simplify and improve benefits access for working families and improve services to individuals with disabilities. The Food Stamp Program should be strengthened to improve benefits, eligibility, and access. And the Temporary Assistance for Needy Families Program should be reformed to shift its focus from cutting caseloads to helping needy families find sustainable employment.

11. **Reduce the high costs of being poor and increase access to financial services.** Despite having less income, lower-income families often pay more than middle- and high-income families for the same consumer products. We recommend that the federal and state governments should address the foreclosure crisis through expanded mortgage-assistance programs and by new federal legislation to curb unscrupulous practices. And we propose that the federal government establish a $50 million Financial Fairness Innovation Fund to support state efforts to broaden access to mainstream goods and financial services in predominantly low-income communities.

(continued)

12. Expand and simplify the Saver's Credit to encourage saving for education, homeownership, and retirement. For many families, saving for purposes such as education, a home, or a small business is key to making economic progress. We propose that the federal "Saver's Credit" be reformed to make it fully refundable. This Credit should also be broadened to apply to other appropriate savings vehicles intended to foster asset accumulation, with consideration given to including individual development accounts, children's saving accounts, and college savings plans.

Source: Center for American Progress (2007). From Poverty to Prosperity: A National Strategy to Cut Poverty in Half. CAP Task Force on Poverty. http://www. americanprogress.org/issues/2007/04/poverty_report.html

food-insecure households, have more diet-related illnesses that also adversely affect their attendance and educational performance, and are more likely to come to school hungry than children with higher socioeconomic status (SES) (ChildStats, 2007). They are more susceptible to asthma and other environmental illnesses because of the living conditions in their neighborhoods, and they are also more likely to have caregivers who are unable to provide homework support (ChildStats, 2007). Finally, they are more likely to be described by their parents and eventually by their teachers as having academic and behavior problems that require intensive intervention, including special education services (ChildStats, 2007; U.S. Census, 2000). This is just a short list of the adverse risk factors associated with living in poverty.

Steps 3 and 4: Appraising and Adapting the Evidence

To contemplate helping children living in poverty in a school setting, a perspective that sees the "big picture" seems to be indicated. It can be overwhelming to realize that you and your school colleagues are a few people, whereas the problems associated with poverty seem massive and even intractable. This is part of the power of the clinical quadrant framework, in my view; it acknowledges that not all problems are ultimately "individual" and require psychological intervention. Rather, interventions in the other three quadrants (combined with support in quadrant C) can go a long way toward making the students and families living in poverty to be better able to access the resources they need and to make the most of their child's educational experience at your school.

In Box 7.1, the Center for American Progress lays out the recommendations of a recent expert panel of policy makers, advocates, and researchers on how U.S. poverty could be cut in half by 2017. There are at least three items on that list that school social workers can begin to apply the clinical quadrant framework to in their school district and at state and local levels. Working to enhance early childhood programs in school districts, advocating for better school-to-work vocational training in high schools, and making higher education a goal for more low-income youth are all activities that school social workers already are involved in working toward. This report underlines the importance of these interventions as they relate to breaking the cycles of poverty that affect so many of the children that school social workers serve.

How to Use the EBP Process to Make Your Whole School Safer, Healthier, and Smarter

It is not enough to exhort school social workers to do more to influence their school on both a micro and macro level: School social workers need to see that the EBP process can be done and is underway in schools across the country. Using case vignettes, this chapter will describe how school social workers assessed the needs of their schools and used an EBP process (with their school as "the client") to design and implement school-wide programs that address complex and multifaceted school problems such as school bullying, depression prevention, and increased social-emotional learning (SEL). As these vignettes indicate, this EBP approach is highly adaptable to a variety of school contexts, and school social workers can use it to mobilize support from administrators, faculty colleagues, and parents to change schools in dramatic and positive ways.

What Are the Major School Climate/Whole-School Issues That Most Affect Student Learning?

In surveying their own and others' prevention work with youth, Tolan, Guerra, and Kendall (1995) identify three different levels of interventions that schools can choose from to try to prevent bullying behavior and school violence:

1. *Universal interventions*: Interventions that are school wide, which focus on curriculum change as well as community programs and involvement for parents and other community stakeholders
2. *Selective interventions*: Programs that focus on specific at-risk students, often employing classroom or group

therapy interventions, which focus on a group for students in a self-contained behavior disorder classroom or on mentoring programs for students who have limited family support

3. *Indicator interventions*: Programs that are directed at students and families who already are showing some signs of having a specific problem such as a student who has already been suspended for fighting or for threatening another student with a weapon (Tolan, Guerra, & Kendall, 1995).

We have seen this framework already in Chapter 6, with the response to intervention (RTI) programs currently underway in many schools, and can now see how it is used to address issues that might adversely impact the entire school community. For this chapter, I will draw from my experience in K-12 schools to describe the three different times I used an EBP process in collaboration with students, administrators, teachers, and parents to implement programs that addressed the school community at multiple levels of intervention, including the macro level.

Several recent school social work literature reviews (Astor et al., 2003; Erickson, Mattaini, & McGuire, 2004; Newsome & Kelly, 2006) discuss some of the most promising universal programs to prevent bullying behavior and school violence. However, although all of the programs noted by their studies have shown some strong initial results in decreasing behavior problems, they are not all conclusively shown to be effective with all schools and all settings, an issue highlighted by the high standards for effectiveness modeled by the Colorado Blueprints for School Violence (CSPV, 2007). Despite such issues, Erickson et al. (2004) note in their review of existing school violence prevention programs that

> The route to significant decreases in the incidence of violence, threat coercion, and other antisocial behaviors does not appear to be through intensive treatment of a few damaged individuals, nor do individuals as vectors of antisocial behavior appear to be a promising route for prevention.
>
> Erickson et al., 2004, p. 36

Although all of the many programs noted by these literature reviews have shown some strong initial results in decreasing behavior problems, the outcomes from the literature do not yet point toward one overarching effective program or treatment model (Newsome & Kelly, 2006). Although the selective and indicator-based programs have been shown to help individual students, these programs thus far have not shown any discernible impact on overall rates of bullying behavior and school violence (Erickson et al., 2004). Additionally, no large-scale studies that utilize all three approaches in one program to address issues of bullying behavior and school violence have been conducted so far, making it hard to know whether a universal, selective, and indicator-based approach would yield the best results (Astor et al., 2003; CASEL, 2005; Greenberg et al., 2003).

Despite some strong indicators that universal intervention programs rooted in community needs and contexts work best and last longest in helping prevent bullying behavior and school violence (CSPV, 2007), the trend in this area of school-based mental health practice seems to be moving toward more selective and indicated interventions that focus on students who are considered at risk. As Astor et al. (2003) state, "from an intervention perspective, it is philosophically problematic that most current school violence interventions and programs are moving away from developing grassroots and community generated interventions" (p. 169).

These school-based prevention and intervention programs, as diverse as they are, focus on the individual student who is either already diagnosed with conduct problems or is considered at risk for having these problems. The assumption of these programs seems to be as follows: Fix the most troubled students in the school, and the school will become overall a safer place. The only problem with this thinking is that the researchers who have demonstrated the effectiveness of their targeted interventions haven't also demonstrated that the overall school climate has improved (Erickson et al., 2004; Mytton et al., 2002). In effect, they are only preventing (possibly) the most troubled students in school from re-offending; although this is certainly good, it's not clear that this is enough. The FBI found that many of the students who committed mass murder in their schools in the late 1990s were involved in group and individual treatments prior to their violent acts and had told classmates about their plans to hurt others (FBI, 2000).

Mediators, Cultural Celebrations, and Kickball: The EBP Process in Action

For my K-6 school, my principal and I saw a strong need to address how our lunchtime was going. Really, it was how it wasn't going that bothered us the most: Both of us noticed after a particularly tough month that we were spending at least an hour or two every day after lunch cleaning up the messes and fights that had taken place on our playground. Given our school's affluent population and low level of behavior problems, it had taken us some time to see the pattern: After all, wasn't our school one of those "good" schools that didn't have problems like bullying and fighting?

Looking over my principal's discipline records and my clinical notes, we were able to target the specific populations that seemed to be in what I called "heavy rotation." The third- and sixth-grade classes had a high number of kids in conflict, and the other major players in the conflicts appeared to be the boys from a self-contained special education class. The conflicts involving these kids was further intensified by the fact that they were the only kids in the entire school who were bused to school, and with the exception of one boy, they were all Latino and African American in a school that was 85% white. Although not all of their conflicts with the other grades involved a racial element, it seemed that we needed to address their possible feelings of cultural alienation in our school if we were to engage them in some problem solving to address the bullying.

My principal and I settled on an EBP question for me to explore (step 1 of the EBP process), "What are the characteristics of effective bullying-prevention programs in elementary schools?" Based on my review of the anti-bullying literature for elementary programs (steps 2 and 3 of the EBP process), we learned that a survey could be a good assessment tool to figure out what areas of the school had the most challenges with bullying (Orpinas, Horne, & Staniszewski, 2003; Astor, Benbenishty, & Meyer, 2004). We then conducted a survey of our school population (step 4 of the EBP process). We designed a short survey for all our K-6-grade-level students (using pictures for the younger grades in our school), our school parents, and our faculty to complete. From this survey we learned the following:

1. Our school community (students, parents, and faculty) did not report violence or racial/sexual harassment as major concerns in our school community.
2. Parents and students both identified cliques and excluding as the major ways that students felt bullied at our school.
3. A majority of our faculty reported witnessing very little bullying behavior and several wondered in our survey's comments section why we were focusing on bullying at "our school."

From our survey data, we convened focus groups of students, particularly the ones in the third, sixth, and special education classrooms (more of step 4 of the EBP process). In these discussions, we were able to implement other aspects that I had found in the literature on effective bullying-prevention programs (Erickson et al., 2004), including asking the students to help us brainstorm ways by which we can best help the school's playground be turned into a more fun and safe place. The students, not surprisingly, had plenty of great ideas, including many we eventually implemented. The best one was our creating a "Peace Team" of older students who I trained in conflict-resolution skills over the course of several lunch periods. The students even took it upon themselves to map the conflicts they saw happen in an average week on our playground (Astor et al., 2004). These students wore reflective vests that identified them as "Peace Teamers" and roamed the playground helping students settle conflicts. The students enjoyed the work, and as with many other studies of peer-mediation programs, we were able to benefit from the advantage of having students seeking help from other students (Newsome & Kelly, 2006). Our discipline records reflected a positive change in student referrals, and in additional focus groups at the end of the year students told us that they thought the program had helped them solve their problems outside on the playground before they needed adult intervention (step 5 of the EBP process).

One challenge in my school's anti-bullying efforts was how to involve the whole-school community, specifically our faculty. Evidence on effective bullying-prevention programs shows that faculty have to be directly engaged in modeling the positive behaviors the students are expected to adopt (Newsome & Kelly, 2006). We organized a working group to help design our survey, and the group offered several great suggestions for interventions that might improve our playground, including an intramural lunchtime sports league based on sportsmanship. The other teachers in the working group committee volunteered to help lead the sports league, and one teacher had a great idea about how we would "keep score." Because so many of our students played competitive sports, and because so many of them had trouble resolving conflicts during games, we instituted a kickball league where we kept no score but asked them to give themselves a 1 to 10 sportsmanship score after the game. We then had each of the top teams play in sportsmanship playoffs and asked each class to nominate the "best sport" for their class for a sportsmanship all-star game. For this game, one of our working group members got so involved in the program that he brought his sound effects CD, and we used a school sound system to play baseball songs and cheers during the all-star game. Even though only 20 students were chosen for the game, 100 students came and cheered their classmates on.

Depression Prevention in a Middle School: EBP in Action

In the year after the Columbine school shootings, my middle school faculty was on edge. We hadn't had any violent incidents, but somehow my colleagues didn't see that: They just kept telling our administrative team and me how we had to "do something" about the kinds of kids that might become violent at our school. Our dean proposed we adopt a profiling software program that would allow us to anticipate who the next school shooter would be, and our student services team discussed buying the software program for two weeks in a row. I was horrified at the idea of all our students having to sit and take a computer-assisted software program that claimed it could identify the dangerous kids. I was also sure that though our administration and faculty might support it, that the parent community might be concerned about the adoption of the program and its potential impact on our school's morale.

Therefore, I went about doing an EBP process on behalf of the school, asking, "What are the characteristics of school shooters?" and "What are the programs that might help address some of the potential risk factors teenagers exhibit that might make them at risk for engaging in violent school behavior?" (step 1 of the EBP process). I found some interesting literature right away, including an FBI intensive study of the school shootings entitled, "The School Shooter: A Threat Assessment Perspective." This report (available at www.fbi.gov/publications/school/school2.pdf) represented the systematic review of previous school shootings by FBI experts and scholars in psychology, criminal justice, and social work. These experts wrote that the kids who became school shooters had a behavior that was based on their personality, family dynamics, and school and social factors, but no one factor was entirely predictive of their eventually becoming violent (FBI, 2000). The need to create school communities where students trust teachers enough to tell them about rumors or threats they've heard, and where students and families who have mental health problems can get help, was also mentioned as a factor in the report. This factor has been supported by subsequent research on positive school climate (Mattaini, 2006; Newsome & Kelly, 2006) (steps 2 and 3 of the EBP process).

I shared these findings with our administrative team, and to my surprise, they asked me to think about how we might start to look first at changing our school climate before going forward with the school shooter software program (step 4 of the EBP process). My assistant principal offered to work with me to build on the peer-mediation program we already had underway and to see if we could explore programs to target students at risk for anger problems and/or violence. We started looking into evidence on programs for those kids, but soon realized that many of those kids were already students whom we knew well and to whom we were giving some assistance (indeed, this may have been one of the reasons we hadn't had any violent events at our school). What stood out to us was some research we saw about programs to prevent alienation and depression. One program, the Penn Resiliency Program (PRP), had shown some ability to prevent students' depressive symptoms after being compared to a control group (Seligman, 1995). The PRP intervention used exercises, discussions, and role-plays to teach students basic cognitive-therapy skills like disputing negative thoughts and using relaxation and other meditation techniques to avoid negative and impulsive behaviors in conflicts with peers. The program's emphasis on problem-solving and cognitive-behavioral interventions appealed to us, and we quickly found several teachers who wanted to pilot the intervention in their classroom. (For more information on the PRP, contact Investigators and Co-Directors: Jane Gillham, Ph.D., & Karen Reivich, Ph.D. e-mail: info@pennproject.org)

One immediate problem with adapting PRP to our school was deciding when to offer the intervention. Many of the PRP schools had done the intervention after school, and based on our prior experience with after school activities, we knew that many of our students would not attend because of their childcare responsibilities, that is, watching their younger siblings (this was particularly true of our Mexican American students, a population we were eager to target with the PRP intervention). This was the pre-NCLB era, but the standards movement had hit our school district hard, and some of our teachers worried about having time to do the 12 sessions in addition to covering all their course material. We opted for lunchtime, and teachers volunteered to lead groups in their classrooms. The next challenge was recruiting students. Fortunately, I had already begun a popular peer-mediation program a few years earlier, with many of the same teachers who had volunteered to lead the PRP, and using those connections with students, we soon had a number of groups ready to go. I led a group, along with our assistant principal, and we paid attention to recruiting students who we felt might be at risk for depression as well as students who just seemed interested in joining the group.

And then...the school year ended, without any incident. In that sense, I can say that the program "worked." However, like many an intervention I've either participated in or been a witness to in K-12 education, we didn't make an evaluation plan to measure the outcome of our program. Ultimately, what I can say the program did is restricted to anecdotes, most of which are positive: students referring themselves and others for counseling, based on their learning on how to recognize the warning signs of depression and negative thinking; parents thanking me at graduation and in the community for "giving my daughter hope"; and students asking me the next year, "are we going to do that lunchtime group again?" We did do another round of the PRP group, this time focusing on our school's self-contained special education classrooms. I continued working at the school for another year before moving to a school closer to my home, and we had no violence at our school the next year either. Looking back at the experience, I realize now that I could have made a better impact on our school's climate if I had used the evidence on depression prevention to follow through to step 5 of the EBP process (evaluating the results) by tracking group and student outcomes, and possibly even by applying for grant funding to bring more SEL programming to our school.

8

■ ■ ■

EBP Is Just the Beginning: Defining a National School Social Work Practice and Research Agenda

This concluding chapter will tie together the threads of the previous seven chapters and argues that EBP is an approach that can ultimately help school social work both increase its effectiveness and resolve (at least some of) its identity crisis. By making school social work practice more reliant on evidence than the more traditional "authority-based" models of practice, school social workers are able to both focus more directly on what clients actually want to change and bring the best available evidence to bear on designing an intervention with their clients. While EBP is certainly already recognized within other areas of social work practice, it is still relatively new in school social work. Learning more about both what EBP is and how it can be applied in practical, real-world situations can potentially help school social workers become partners with policymakers and researchers to conduct intervention studies that help practitioners answer the questions they and their clients are most concerned about answering. While EBP is no magic cure for what ails school social work, it does provide a framework to reimagine what school social work can be in this new era of accountability that is both outcome informed and sensitive to specific client needs.

Where Are We Going, and How Can EBP Help Us Get There?

In preparing this book, I found this poignant quote from the *Elementary School Journal*, May 1958:

> The school social worker can help only a few children at a time. Who will they be? How will they be selected?...It is the responsibility of the school social worker to make know the lack of essential services and their effect on children and families. It is also the responsibility of the school social worker to help people fuse their efforts to fill the gap and prevent tragedies that interfere with children's schooling.
>
> Mitchell, 1958, pp. 440-441

How much has changed with the challenges faced by school social workers, nearly 50 years later? Maybe our "tragedies" are different than the ones Mitchell wrote of in 1958, but the challenges remain. Fortunately, we now have the ability to harness the best available evidence to help us try to meet these needs. With the EBP process that has been taught and demonstrated in this book, school social workers have a chance to begin to have a larger impact on the schools they serve.

Today, most school social workers are at least able to give intensive help to at least 20 to 50 children per week, most of who have individualized education plans (IEPs). However, despite the high job satisfaction noted, for example, by my Illinois study sample, it seems that many outside sources (e.g., teachers, administrators, and IEP teams) still largely determine the school social workers' client loads and the IEP-related terms of this client work. The challenge that this research poses for school social workers will be to see whether they can take their clear passion for serving students and maintain the profession's strength as it enters this uncertain new era of No Child Left Behind (NCLB), EBP, and outcome-based education.

In terms of the actual practice choices preferred by Illinois school social workers and the limited data available in other states, their choices are reflective of at least some of the current literature on the best practice in the field. The four major reviews of effective school social work practice presently available (Early & Vonk, 2001; Sabatino, Mayer, & Timberlake, 2006; Franklin et al., 2006; Staudt et al., 2005) were present in the responses of over 50% of my Illinois study's respondents. For example, in the vignettes about the aggressive and anxious students, over 65% of the school social worker respondents chose cognitive-behavior therapy (CBT) as one of their treatment options; 85% said that they would collaborate closely with the angry student's teacher to develop and monitor a behavior contract. For the students with Asperger's syndrome, persistent shyness, and anxiety, at least 70% of school social worker respondents chose interventions that involved working directly with parents and teachers in addition to working with the child in a more traditional clinical context. All of these interventions have strong empirical backing and would likely make some contribution to resolving these students' issues in the majority of cases (Franklin et al., 2006).

That a significant majority of the study's respondents chose at least one intervention rooted in EBP for each vignette is encouraging; however, what is more concerning is that almost the same percentage seemed to pick "ongoing weekly counseling and support for the student" as one of their other intervention options. (Given the nature of the survey—asking school social workers to self-report on practice options they had used in the past without prioritizing them—there is no way to know which intervention they used most often for each vignette.) That said, in Illinois, where 68% of school social workers report that at least half of their caseload is composed of students getting mandated IEP services, the implications of this consistent pattern of picking ongoing counseling as a major practice choice are serious. By choosing "ongoing weekly counseling" as the most popular option in nearly every clinical vignette, Illinois school social workers might be simply going with what they're most comfortable. They might believe that this is the most effective treatment option, though evidence tends to favor briefer, problem-focused treatments (Constable, 2006; Early & Vonk, 2001; Franklin, 1999; Franklin et al., 2006; Newsome, 2004).

But whatever the reason, if "ongoing counseling" is really the choice they favor most, many Illinois school social workers are virtually guaranteeing themselves a limited reach and scope in their practice environment because "ongoing counseling" on top of mandated IEP minutes will quickly shrink the available time they have to do classroom groups or other prevention-based programmatic interventions. Additionally, factoring in the fact that 44% of school social workers in Illinois reported doing more than 6 hours of IEP-related paperwork, the picture of Illinois school social work comes sharper into focus.

In addition to research showing the benefit of designing school-wide prevention programs for students, school social workers nationwide are being increasingly required to demonstrate their effectiveness in helping students meet academic and behavioral standards (Browder & Cooper-Duffy, 2003: Clark, 1990; Dupper, 2003; Franklin, 1999; Newsome, 2004). The passage of NCLB has only increased the pressure on all educators to show that their interventions improve students' academic performance. A comprehensive national survey of school social workers seems to be a good place to start in building the infrastructure of school social work practice for the 21st century. It is my hope that this book is only the beginning in enhancing and enlarging school social work's role in America's schools.

There are three implications from the research and concepts in this book, one each for practice, social work education, and future research.

Practice Implications

School social work practitioners need to be on balance encouraged by the findings in this book and need to use these findings to enhance and expand their roles in their schools. School social work, in Illinois and in many other regions of the country, is a growing profession, full of practitioners with a wealth of experience who are often "lifers" in their school district and who have responded again and again to some of the most challenging situations social workers can face. They have assumed this responsibility in a "host environment" that doesn't necessarily understand their role as school social workers, and they have managed to fashion an identity that is stable and positive enough such that a full 93% of Illinois school social workers would sign up for this profession all over again if given a chance to start over.

Yet with this stability comes the risk of complacency and overconfidence. Most practitioners in Illinois reported thinking that they had received adequate training in EBP, yet many fewer respondents actually demonstrated that they knew how to access EBP databases or in fact choose empirically validated interventions that might increase their practice effectiveness and save them time. Now that this survey has shown some initial signs that organizational variables within schools themselves are not going to be the key predictors of whether school social workers continue to move toward more innovative clinical and systemic practice, it is up to school social workers to use their individual and collective power as professionals to advocate for increased expansion of school social work services in their districts that extend beyond the traditional IEP-based model. One of the first ways to do this is to embrace intervention models like the 3-tier model described in this book or the clinical quadrant framework also described in detail in these pages. Using these frameworks will help us think more creatively and clearly about the best places to intervene, and then using the EBP process described here, we will be able to collaborate with clients to use the best available evidence to help them.

Training Implications

Constable and Alvarez (2006) recount how Indiana has instituted a school social worker/university/state board of education partnership to develop an advanced specialization requirement for school social workers graduating from Master of Social Work (MSW) programs in Indiana. Like in Illinois, school social worker graduates in Indiana will be granted MSW but, in contrast, will be given a probationary 3-year school social work certificate to practice in Indiana schools. From year 1 to year 3, they will be assigned senior school social worker mentors (not in their district) who will provide guidance and additional training in some of the issues outlined in this research project. They will be expected to develop and implement a wide array of practice interventions and treatment modalities, at the same time honing their skills of using EBP and cultural competence to design both individual and whole-school interventions.

Finally, all Indiana school social workers will be expected to maintain and create a portfolio that demonstrates that they have learned how to evaluate their own work and integrate a range of practice interventions ranging from indicator interventions to universal prevention programs. This will be the first advanced specialization school social work certificate of its kind in the nation and will represent Indiana's response to federal requirements that all educators (including school social workers) should demonstrate that they are "highly qualified" (Constable & Alvarez, 2006). On consulting with Constable last year, he shared that the catalyst for all this work was his own unpublished statewide survey of Indiana school social workers (R. Constable, personal communication, July 20, 2006).

These ideas are not isolated to Indiana. In Ohio, a recent focus group research was conducted by Dawn Anderson-Butcher and her team at Ohio State to help inform potential post-master's advanced training for school social workers (Anderson-Butcher & Kelly, manuscript under review). Additionally, at our Family and Schools Partnership Program (FSPP) at Loyola, we have started a post-master's certificate program closely based on some of the same ideas underway in Indiana, and will have our first "graduating" class in June 2008.

The FSPP was created to help Chicago area's school-based mental health professionals provide more effective services in the schools, prekindergarten to 12th grade, in which they work. The FSPP approach stresses the importance of strengthening the system in which students function, emphasizing team building and collaboration among students, families, school staff, and the larger community. The model encourages professionals to help students and families identify and build on their strengths, instead of emphasizing deficits. The primary focus of the FSPP is on "whole school intervention," helping professionals see the "whole school system" as the focus of their work. Within that framework, the program provides professionals with practical knowledge and skills to help students at high risk of dropout, failure, and serious behavior problems, as well as students in the regular school program, overcome obstacles to academic success and healthy psychosocial development. The FSPP is built on the belief that there is a wealth of gifted professionals already in schools who, with intensive training, support, networking, and immersion in systemically oriented strength based strategies, can become more effective practitioners and dynamic leaders for systemic change. (For more information, see the FSPP Web site http://www.luc.edu/socialwork/fspp.shtml.)

Research Implications

Franklin's call for building school social work's infrastructure now has another small addition to its foundation (Franklin, 2001b). Along with the work Constable and others are doing in Indiana, as well as some exciting new school social work associations growing in Louisiana, New Jersey, Maryland, and California, there is a potential for a renaissance in school social workers' practice. However, such notions of rebirth will be just rhetoric unless rigorous and relevant school social work intervention research continues. Staudt et al. (2005) found that many of the studies of school social work effectiveness in the literature lacked sufficient scientific rigor. One hopeful outcome of this research project would be a renewed focus on developing researcher-practitioner relationships all across the country where many of the interventions described in this project could be rigorously tested against each other and a database of successful treatment interventions could be developed and maintained for all school social workers to consult. The need is clear; the question now will be whether the key players in school social work will rise to the challenge.

References

Abbott, A. (1988). *The system of professions: An essay on the division of expert labor.* Chicago: University of Chicago Press.

Allen-Meares, P. (1977). Analysis of tasks. *Social Work, 22*(3), 196-201.

Allen-Meares, P. (1993). Pull and push: Clinical or macro interventions in schools. *Social Work in Education, 15*(1), 3-5.

Allen-Meares, P. (1994). Social work services in schools: A national study of entry-level tasks. *Social Work, 39*(5), 560-566.

Allen-Meares, P. (2004). *Social work services in schools* (4th ed.). Boston: Allyn & Bacon.

Allen-Meares, P. (2007). *Social work services in schools* (5th ed.). Boston: Allyn & Bacon.

Altshuler, S. (2006). Professional requirements for school social work and other school mental health professions. In C. Franklin, M. Harris, & P. Allen-Meares (Eds.), *School services sourcebook.* New York: Oxford Press.

Altshuler, S., & Kopels, S. (2003). Advocating in schools for children with disabilities: What's new with IDEA? *Social Work, 48*(3), 320-329.

Amato, P. R. (2000). Consequences of divorce for adults and children. *Journal of Marriage and the Family, 62,* 1269-1287.

American Psychiatric Association. (2000). *Diagnostic and Statistical Manual of Mental Disorders (DSM-IV-TR).* Arlington, VA: APPI Press.

Anderson, L. W. (2005, April 4). The No Child Left Behind Act and the legacy of federal aid to education. *Education Policy Analysis Archives, 13*(24). Retrieved June 1, 2007, from http://epaa.asu.edu/epaa/v13n24/

Anderson-Butcher, D., & Ashton, D. (2004). Innovative models of collaboration to serve children, youths, families, and communities. *Children & Schools, 26*(1), 39-53.

Anderson-Butcher, D., Iachini, A., & Wade-Mdivanian, R. (2007). *School linkage protocol technical assistance guide: Expanded school improvement through the enhancement of the learning support continuum.* Columbus, OH: College of Social Work, Ohio State University.

Anderson-Butcher, D., & Kelly, M. *Focus group and pilot survey data on school social work Practice.* Manuscript under review.

Andrews, R. L., & Soder, R. (1987). Principal leadership and student achievement. *Educational Leadership, 44*(6), 9-11.

Anxiety Disorders Association of America. (2007). Medications for anxiety disorders. Retrieved August 28, 2007, from http://www.adaa.org/gettinghelp/AnxietyDisorders/Medications.asp

Astor, R., Behre, W. J., Wallace, J. M., & Fravil, K. A. (1998). School social workers and school violence: Personal safety, training, and violence programs. *Social Work, 43,* 223-232.

Astor, R., Benbenishty, R., & Marachi, R. (2006). Violence in schools. In P. Allen-Meares (Ed.), *Social work services in schools* (pp. 145-170). New York: Allyn & Bacon.

Astor, R., Benbenishty, R., & Meyer, H. A. (2004). Monitoring and mapping student victimization in schools. *Theory Into Practice, 43*(1), 39-49.

Balon, R. (2007). Rating scales for anxiety/anxiety disorders. *Current Psychiatry Reports, 9*(4), 271-277.

Barnett, D. W., Daly, E. J., III, Jones, K. M., & Lentz, F. E., Jr. (2004). Response to intervention. *Journal of Special Education, 38*(2), 66-79.

Bentley, K. J., & Collins, K. S. (2006). Psychopharmacological treatment for child and adolescent mental disorders. In C. Franklin, M. B. Harris, & P. Allen-Meares (Eds.), *School services sourcebook.* New York: Oxford University Press.

Bowen, G. L., & Richman, J. M. (2001). *School success profile.* Chapel Hill, NC: Jordan Institute for Families, School of Social Work, The University of North Carolina at Chapel Hill.

Browder, D. M., & Cooper-Duffy, K. (2003). What is special about special education? Evidence-based practices for students with severe disabilities and the requirement for accountability in "No Child Left Behind." *The Journal of Special Education, 37*(3), 157-164.

Caldarella, P., & Merrell, K. (1997). Common dimensions of social skills of children and adolescents: A taxonomy of positive behaviors. *School Psychology Review, 26*(2), 264-279.

Camacho, M., & Hunter, L. (2006). Effective interventions for students with separation anxiety disorder. In C. Franklin, M. Harris, & P. Allen-Meares (Eds.), *School services sourcebook.* New York: Oxford Press.

Carr-Saunders, A. P., & Wilson, P. A. (1933). *The professions.* Oxford: Oxford University Press.

CASEL. (2007). What is SEL. Retrieved May 30, 2007, from http://www.casel.org/basics/definition.php

Case Western Reserve Engineering Center for Ethics. (2005). Online ethics center. Retrieved February 12, 2006, from http://onlineethics.org/CMS/profpractice.aspx

Center for American Progress. (2007). From poverty to prosperity: A national strategy to cut Poverty in half. CAP Task Force on Poverty. Retrieved August 29, 2007, from www.americanprogress.org/issues/2007/04/poverty_report.html

Center for the Study and Prevention of Violence. (2007). Blueprints for violence prevention Overview. Retrieved August 28, 2007, from http://www.colorado.edu/cspv/blueprints/

ChildStats. (2007). America's children: Key national indicators of well-being, 2007. Retrieved August 18, 2007, from http://www.childstats.gov/americaschildren/

Clark, J. P. (1990). The challenge of demonstrating the outcomes of school social work intervention. *Journal of School Social Work, 4*(2), 55-66.

Collaborative on Social and Emotional Learning (CASEL). (2007). List of best practices for social-emotional learning in schools. Retrieved January 10, 2007, from www.casel.org

Constable, R. (2006). Mandates and beyond. Keynote address, Loyola Family School Partnership Program.

Constable, R., & Alvarez, M. (2006, Summer). Specialization in school social work: The Indiana example. *School Social Work Journal,* 116-132.

Cooke, M. B., Ford, J., Levine, J., Bourke, C., Newell, L., & Lapidus, G. (2007). The effects of city-wide implementation of "Second Step" on elementary school students' prosocial and aggressive behaviors. *The Journal of Primary Prevention, 28*(2), 93-114.

Corcoran, J. (1998). Solution-focused practice with middle and high school at-risk Youths. *Social Work in Education, 20*(4), 232-243.

Costin, L. (1969). School social work: An analysis of function. *Psychology in the Schools, 6*(4), 347-352.

Crespi, T. D., Gustafson, A. L., & Borges, S. M. (2005). Group counseling in the schools: Considerations for child and family issues. *Journal of Applied Psychology, 22*(1), 67-85.

DeLucia-Waack, J. L., & Gerrity, D. (2001). Effective group work for elementary school-age children whose parents are divorcing. *The Family Journal, 9*(3), 273-284.

DIBELS. (2007). Introduction to DIBELS. Retrieved August 11, 2007, from http://dibels.uoregon.edu/index.php

Duncan, B., Hubble, M., & Miller, S. (Eds.) (1999). *Heart and soul of change: What works in therapy.* Washington, DC: American Psychological Association Press.

DuPaul, G. J., & Eckert, T. L. (1997). The effects of school-based interventions for attention-deficit disorder: A meta-analysis. *School Psychology Review, 26*(1), 5-27.

DuPaul, G. J., & Weyandt, L. L. (2006). School-based intervention for children with ADD. *International Journal of Disability, Development and Education, 53*(2), 161-176.

Dupper, D. R. (2003). *School social work: Skills and interventions for effective practice*. Hoboken, NJ: Wiley & Sons.

Dupper, D. R. (2006). Design and utility of life skills groups in schools. In C. Franklin, M. Harris, & P. Allen-Meares (Eds.), *School services sourcebook*. New York: Oxford Press.

Early, T., & Vonk, M. E. (2001). Effectiveness of school social work from a risk and resilience perspective. *Children & Schools, 23*(1), 9-31.

Elliot, D. S. (1998). *Blueprints for violence prevention*. Boulder, CO: Center for the Study and Prevention of Violence: University of Colorado.

Erickson, C. L., Mattaini, M., & McGuire, M. (2004). Constructing nonviolent cultures in schools: The state of the science. *Children & Schools, 26*(2), 102-117.

Essau, C. A., Conradt, J., & Petermann, F. (1999). Frequency of panic attacks and panic disorder in adolescents. *Depression & Anxiety, 9,* 19-26.

Evans, S. W., Pelham, W., & Grudberg, M. V. (1996-1995). The efficacy of note taking to improve behavior and comprehension of adolescents with attention deficit hyperactivity disorder. *Abstract Expectionality, 5*(1), 1-17 (doi: 10.1207/s 15327035ex0501_1).

Evans, S. W., Timmins, B., Sibley, M., Sibley, L., White, C., Serpell, Z. N., et al. (2006). Developing coordinated, multimodal, school-based treatment for young adolescents with ADHD. *Education and Treatment of Children, 29*(2), 359-378.

Fasko, S. N. (2006). Special education services and response to intervention: What, why, and how? *Third Education Group Review/Essays, 2*(9). Retrieved July 1, 2007, from http://www.thirdeducationgroup.org/Review/Essays/v2n9.htm

Federal Bureau of Investigation. (2000). The school shooter: A threat assessment perspective. Retrieved July 3, 2005, from www.fbi.gov/publications/school/school2.pdf

Franklin, C. (2001a). The effectiveness of solution-focused therapy with children in a school setting. *Research on Social Work Practice, 11*(4), 411-434.

Franklin, C. (2001b). Now is the time for building the infrastructure of school social work practice. *Children and Schools, 23,* 67-71.

Franklin, C. (2005). The future of school social work practice: Current trends and opportunities. *Advances in Social work, 6,* 167-181.

Franklin, C., & Gerlach, B. (2006, Summer). One hundred years of linking schools with communities: Current models and opportunities. *School Social Work Journal,* 44-62.

Franklin, C., Harris, M. B., & Allen-Meares, P. (Eds.) (2006). *The school services sourcebook: A guide for social workers, counselors, and mental health professionals.* Oxford: Oxford University Press.

Franklin, C., & Hopson, L. (2004). Into the schools with evidence-based practices. *Children & Schools, 26*(2), 67-70.

Frey, A., & Dupper, D. (2005). Towards a 21st century model of school social work practice. *Children & Schools, 27*(1), 33-44.

Freidson, E. (1986). *Professional powers: A study of the institutionalization of formal knowledge.* Chicago: University of Chicago Press.

Fuchs, L. S., & Fuchs, D. (1998). Treatment validity: A unifying concept for reconceptualizing the identification of learning disabilities. *Learning Disabilities Research & Practice, 13,* 204-219.

Fuchs, L. S., & Fuchs, D. (2001). Principles for sustaining research-based practice in the schools: A case study. *Focus on Exceptional Children, 33*(1), 1-14.

Fuchs, D., Mock, D., Morgan, P., & Young, C. (2003). Responsiveness-to-intervention: Definitions, evidence, and implications for learning disabilities construct. *Learning Disabilities: Research and Practice, 18*(3), 157-171.

Gambrill, E. (2001). Social work: An authority-based profession. *Research on Social Work Practice, 11*(2), 166-175.

Gambrill, E. (2003). Evidence-based practice: Sea change or the emperor's new clothes? *Journal of Social Work Education, 39*(1), 3-23.

Gibbs, L. (2003). *Evidence-based practice for the helping professions.* New York: Brooks/Cole.

Gilgun, J. F. (2005). The four cornerstones of evidence-based practice in social work. *Research on Social Work Practice, 15,* 52-61.

Glasgow, R. E., Klesges, L. M., Dzewaltowski, D. A., Bull, S. S., & Estabrooks, P. A. (2004). The future of health behavior change research: What is needed to improve translation of research into health promotion practice? *Annals of Behavioral Medicine, 27,* 3-12.

Glisson, C. (1992). Structure and technology in human service organizations. In Y. Hershenfeld (Ed.), *Human services as complex organizations.* Thousand Oaks, CA: Sage Publications.

Glisson, C. (2000). Organizational culture and climate. In R. Patti (Ed.), *The handbook of social welfare management* (pp. 195-218). Thousand Oaks, CA: Sage Publications.

Glisson, C., & Hemmelgarn, A. (1998). The effects of organizational climate and interorganizational coordination on the quality and outcomes of children's service systems. *Child Abuse & Neglect, 22*(5), 401-421.

Goleman, D. (1997). *Emotional intelligence: Why it can matter more than IQ.* New York: Bantam Books.

Greenberg, M. Weissberg, R. P., O'Brien, M. U., Zins, J. E., Fredericks, L., Resnik, H., et al. (2003). Enhancing school-based prevention and youth development through coordinated social, emotional, and academic learning. *American Psychologist, 58*(6/7), 466-474.

Greenwood, E. (1962). Attributes of a profession. In S. Nosow & W. Form (Eds.), *Man, work, and society.* New York: Basic Books.

Gresham, F. M. (2002). Responsiveness to intervention: An alternative approach to the identification of learning disabilities. In R. Bradley, L. Danielson, & D. P. Hallahan (Eds.), *Identification of learning disabilities: Response to treatment* (pp. 467-519). Mahwah, NJ: Erlbaum.

Gresham, F. M. (2004). Current status and future directions of school-based behavioral interventions. *School Psychology Review, 33*, 326-343.

Grossman, D. C., Neckerman, H. J., Koepsell, T. D., Liu, P. Y., Asher, K. N., Beland, K., et al. (1997). Effectiveness of a violence prevention curriculum among children in elementary school: A randomized controlled trial. *Journal of the American Medical Association, 277*, 1605-1611.

Haine, R. A., Sandler, I. N., Wolchik, S. A., Tein, J.-Y., & Dawson-McClure, S. R. (2003). Changing the legacy of divorce: Evidence from prevention programs and future directions. *Family Relations, 52*, 397-405.

Han, S. S., Catron, T., Weiss, B., & Marciel, K. K. (2005). A teacher-consultation approach to social skills training for pre-K children: Treatment model and short-term outcome effects. *Journal of Abnormal Child Psychology, 33*(6), 681-693.

Harris, K. R., Graham, S., Reid, R., McElroy, K., & Hamby, R. (1994). Self-monitoring of attention versus self-monitoring of performance: Replication and cross-task comparison. *Learning Disability Quarterly, 17*, 121-139.

Hennessey, B. A. (2006). Promoting social competence in school-aged children: The effects of the open circle program. *Journal of School Psychology, 45*, 349-360.

Heward, W. L. (2003). Ten faulty notions about special education. *The Journal of Special Education, 36*(4), 186-205.

Horn, W. F., & Tynan, D. (2001, Summer). Revamping special education. *Public Interest, 144*, 36-53.

Hubble, M., Duncan, B., & Miller, S. (1999). *The heart and soul of change.* Washington, DC: American Psychological Association Press.

Huxtable, M. (2006). International Network for School Social Work: The Status of School Social Work Results of 2006 survey. Retrieved June 1, 2007, from http://www.hkcss.org.hk/cy/Final%20Report%20 International%20Network%202006.pdf

Illinois Association of School Social Workers. (2005). The history of school social work in Illinois. Retrieved January 3, 2005, from www.iaschool social workers.org

Illinois State Board of Education. (2005). Standards for school service personnel. Retrieved June 1, 2005 from www.isbe.state.il.us

Individuals with Disabilities Education Act. (2004). Questions and answers on RTI. Retrieved July 3, 2007, from http://idea.ed.gov/explore/view/p/%2Croot%2Cdynamic%2CQaCorner%2C8%2C

Jonson-Reid, M., Kontak, D., Citerman, B., Essma, A., & Fezzi, N. (2004). School social work case characteristics, services, and dispositions: Year one results. *Children & Schools, 26*(1), 5-22.

Kelly, M. *School social work practice: Results from a statewide survey.* Manuscript under review.

Kendall, P. C. (1994). Treating anxiety disorders in children: Results of a randomized clinical trial. *Journal of Consulting and Clinical Psychology, 62,* 100-110.

Kendall, P. C., Flannery-Schroeder, E., Panicelli-Mindel, S. M., Southam-Gerow, M. A., Henin, A. A., & Warnam, M. (1997). Therapy for youths with anxiety disorders: A second randomized clinical trial. *Journal of Consulting and Clinical Psychology, 65,* 366-380.

Kendall, P. C., & Hedkte, K. (2006). The coping cat workbook (2nd ed.) (Child Therapy Workbook Series). Ardmore, PA: Workbook Publishing.

Kim, J., & Franklin, C. *School social work meta-analysis.* Manuscript under review.

King, N. J., & Heyne, D. (2000). Promotion of empirically validated psychotherapies in counselling psychology. *Counseling Psychology Quarterly, 13*(1), 1-12.

Ladner, M., & Hammons, C. (2005). Special but unequal: Race and special education. Retrieved August 22, 2007, from http://www.edexcellence.net/library/special_ed/special_ed_ch5.pdf

Larson, M. S. (1977). *The rise of professionalism: A sociological analysis.* Berkeley, CA: University of California Press.

LeCroy, C. W. (2004). Experimental evaluation of the "Go Grrrls" preventive intervention for early adolescent girls. *Journal of Primary Prevention, 25,* 457-473.

Leithwood, K., & Jantzi, D. (1999). The relative effects of principal and teacher sources of leadership on student engagement with school. *Educational Administration Quarterly, 35*(5), 679-706.

Litner, B. (2003). Teens with ADHD: The challenge of high school. *Child & Youth Care Forum, 32,* 137-158.

Losen, D. J., & Orfield, G. (Eds.). (2002). *Racial inequity in special education.* Cambridge, MA: Harvard Press.

Lowry-Webster, H. M., Barrett, P. M., & Dadds, M. R. (2001). A universal prevention trial of anxiety and depressive symptomatology in childhood: Preliminary data from an Australian study. *Behaviour Change, 18,* 36-50.

MacDonald, K. M. (1995). *The sociology of professions.* London: Sage Publications.

Masia-Warner, C., Klein, R. G., Dent, H. C., Fisher, P., Alvir, J., Albano, A. M., et al. (2005). School-based intervention for adolescents with social anxiety disorder: Results of a controlled study. *Journal of Abnormal Child Psychology, 33*(6), 707-722.

Massat, C., Orenstein, E., & Moses, H. (2006). Mental health and school social work. In R. Constable, C. Massat, S. McDonald, & J. Flynn (Eds.), *School social work: Practice, policy, and research.* Chicago: Lyceum.

McConnell, R. A., & Sim, A. J. (2000). Evaluating an innovating counselling service for children of divorce. *British Journal of Guidance and Counselling, 28*(1), 75-86.

McGlynn, E. A., Asch, S. M., & Adams, J. (2003). The quality of health care delivered to adults in the United States. *New England Journal of Medicine, 348,* 2635-2645.

Metropolitan Area Child Study. (2007). FCRG publication list. Retrieved August 10, 2007, from http://www.psych.uic.edu/fcrg/publications.html

Mifsud, C., & Rapee, R. M. (2005). Early intervention for childhood anxiety in a school setting: Outcomes for an economically disadvantaged population. *Journal of American Academy Child Adolescent Psychiatry, 44*(10), 996-1004.

Millerson, G. (1964). *The qualifying associations.* London: Routledge.

Mitchell, G. (1958). When to prescribe the school social worker. *The Elementary School Journal, 58*(8), 439-444.

Morrison, V. (May, 2004). School social work in Illinois. *IASSW News.*

Mytton, J. A., DiGuiseppi, C., Gough, D. A., Taylor, R. S., & Logan, S. (2002). School-based violence prevention trials: Systematic review of secondary prevention trials. *Archives of Pediatric Adolescent Medicine, 156,* 752-762.

National Association of Social Workers. (2002). NASW Standards for school social work practice. Retrieved July 10, 2007, from http://www.socialworkers.org/practice/standards/NASW_SSWS.pdf

National Association of Social Workers. (1999). Code of ethics. Retrieved August 28, 2003, from http://www.socialworkers.org/pubs/code/code.asp

National Longitudinal Transition Study. (1993). First wave data. Retrieved July 15, 2007, from http://www.nlts2.org/links.html

National Marriage Project. (2006). The state of our unions: The social health of marriage in America, 2005. Retrieved July 20, 2007, from http://marriage.rutgers.edu/Publications/SOOU/SOOU2006.pdf

Newsome, S. (2002). *The effectiveness and utility of solution-focused brief therapy (SFBT) with at-risk junior high students: A quasi-experimental study.* Unpublished dissertation.

Newsome, S. (2004). Solution-focused interventions with at-risk students: Enhancing the bottom line. *Research on Social Work Practice, 14*(5), 336-343.

Newsome, S., & Kelly, M. (2006). School violence and bullying: Best practice interventions. In J. Waller (Ed.), *Child and adolescent mental health in the classroom.* Thousand Oaks, CA: Sage Publications.

No Child Left Behind. (2002). Introduction to the NCLB legislation. Retrieved February 20, 2004, from http://www.ed.gov/nclb/overview/intro/4pillars.html

Nylund, D. (2000). *Treating Huckleberry Finn: A new narrative approach to working with kids diagnosed ADD/ADHD.* San Francisco: Jossey-Bass.

Orpinas, P., Horne, A. M., & Staniszewski, D. (2003). School bullying: Changing the problem by changing the school. *School Psychology Review, 32*(3), 431-445.

Oswald, D. P., & Mazefsky, C. A. (2006). Empirically supported psychotherapy interventions for internalizing disorders. *Psychology in the Schools, 43*(4), 439-449.

Pascopella, A. (2003). The next challenge. *District Administration, 39*(6), 24-30.

Pedro-Carroll, J. L., Sutton, S. E., & Wyman, P. A. (1999). A two-year follow-up evaluation of a preventive intervention for young children of divorce. *School Psychology Review, 28*(3), 467-476.

Perlstadt, H. (1998). Commentary on Turner. *Sociological Perspectives, 41*(2), 259-273.

Peterson, K. (2002). The professional development of principals: Innovations and opportunities. *Educational Administration Quarterly, 38*(2), 213-232.

President's Commission on Excellence in Special Education (2002). *A New Era: Revitalizing Special Education for Children and their families.* Retrieved on July 10, 2007, from http://www.ed.gov/inits/commissionsboards/whspecialeducatiar/reports/index.html

Presidential New Freedom Commission on Mental Health. (2002). Final Report. Retrieved August 15, 2007, from http://www.mentalhealthcommission.gov/reports/reports.htm

Raines, J. (2004). Evidence-based practice in school social work: A process in perspective. *Children & Schools, 26*(2), 71-85.

Raines, J. (2006, Summer). SWOT! A strategic plan for school social work in the 21st century. *School Social Work Journal,* 132-150.

Raines, J. (2007). *Evidence-based practice in schools.* Presentation at School Social Work Association of America, April 2007.

Reid, R., Trout, A. L., & Schartz, M. (2005). Self-regulation interventions for children with ADHD. *Exceptional Children, 71*(4), 361-377.

Reschly, D. (2004). Commentary: Paradigm shift, outcomes criteria, and behavioral interventions: Foundations for the future of school psychology. *School Psychology Review, 33,* 408-416.

Rich, B. W., Molloy, P., Hart, B., Ginsberg, S., & Mulvey, T. (2007). Conducting a children's divorce group: One approach. *Journal of Child and Adolescent Nursing, 20*(3), 163-175.

Robison, L. M., Sclar, D. A., Skaer, T. L., & Galin, R. S. (1999). National trends in the prevalence attention deficit/hyperactivity disorder and the prescribing of methylphenidate among school-age children: 1990-1995. *Clinical Pediatrics, 38*(4), 209-217.

Sabatino, C. A., Mayer, L. M., & Timberlake, E. M. (2006). The effectiveness of school social work practice. In R. Constable, C. Massat, S. McDonald, & J. Flynn (Eds.), *School social work: Practice, policy, and research.* Chicago: Lyceum.

Sackett, D. L., Rosenberg, W. M. C., Gray, J. A. M., Haynes, R. B., & Richardson, W. D. (1996). Evidence based medicine: What it is and what it isn't. *British Medical Journal, 312,* 71-72.

SAMHSA. (2007). National mental health information center: Anxiety disorders. Retrieved August 20, 2007, from http://mentalhealth.samhsa.gov/publications/allpubs/ken98-0045/default.asp

School Social Work Association of America. (2005). State-by-state information on school social workers. Retrieved January 10, 2005, from www.school social workersaa.org

Seligman, M. (1995). *The optimistic child.* New York: Harper Paperbacks.

Shaffer, G. (2007). Promising school social work practices of the 1920s: Reflections for today. *Children & Schools, 28*(4), 243-251.

Shriver, T. P., & Weissberg, R. P. (August 16, 2005). No emotion left behind. *New York Times,* 31.

Shure, M. B., & Spivack, G. (1982). Interpersonal problem-solving in young children: A cognitive approach to prevention. *American Journal of Community Psychology, 10*(3), 341-356.

Smith, R. (2004). Saving black boys. *American Prospect, 15*(2), 49-50.

Staudt, M., Cherry, D. J., & Watson, M. (2005). Practice guidelines for school social workers: A modified replication of a prototype. *Children & Schools, 27*(2), 71-81.

Stevens, J. W. (1999). Creating collaborative partnerships: Clinical intervention research in an inner-city middle school. *Social Work in Education, 21*(3), 151.

Stolberg, A., & Mahler, J. (1994). Enhancing treatment gains in a school-based intervention for children of divorce. *Journal of Consulting and Clinical Psychology, 62*(1), 147-156.

Stone, S., & Gambrill, E. (2007). Do school social work texts provide a sound guide for practice and policy? *Children & Schools, 29*(2), 109-118.

Swanson, H. Z., Harris, K. R., & Graham, S. (2005). *Handbook of learning disabilities.* New York: Guilford Press.

Teasley, M. (2006). Effective treatments for attention deficit disorder. In C. Franklin, M. Harris, & P. Allen-Meares (Eds.), *School services sourcebook.* New York: Oxford Press.

Teasley, M., Baffour, T. D., & Tyson, E. H. (2005). Perceptions of cultural competence among urban school social workers: Does experience make a difference? *Children & Schools, 27*(4), 227-236.

Thyer, B. A., & Myers, L. L. (1999). On science, antiscience, and the client's right to effective treatment. *Social Work, 44*(5), 501-504.

Tip O'Neill, T. P., & Hymel, G. (1995). *All politics is local: And other rules of the game.* Holbrook, MA: B. Adams.

Tolan, P., & Guerra, N. (1995). What works in reducing adolescent violence: An empirical review of the field. Monograph prepared for the Center for the Study And Prevention of Youth Violence. Boulder, CO: University of Colorado.

Tolan, P., Guerra, N., & Kendall, P. (1995). A developmental-ecological perspective on antisocial behavior in children and adolescents: Toward a unified risk and intervention framework. *Journal of Consulting and Clinical Psychology, 63*(4), 579-584.

Torres, A. (1998). The status of school social work. In E. Freeman & C. Franklin (Eds.), *Multisystem skills and interventions in school social work practice* (pp. 461-470). Washington, DC: NASW.

United States Department of Education. (2005). *Information on no child left behind.* Retrieved January 12, 2006, from www.ed.gov

United States House Committee on Education and the Workforce, (October 21, 2001). *Overidentification issues within the individuals with disabilities education act and the need for reform* (ED Publication No. 473013). Washington, DC: Government Printing Office.

Van Acker, R.., Boreson, L., Gable, R. A., & Potterton, T. (2005). Are we on the right course? Lessons learned about current FBA/BIP practices in schools. *Journal of Behavioral Education, 14*(1), 35-56.

Walker, H. (2004). Commentary: Use of evidence-based interventions in schools: Where we've been, where we are, and where we need to go. *School Psychology Review, 33,* 398-407.

Walker, H. M., & Gresham, F. M. (2003). School-related behavior disorders. In W. M. Reynolds & G. Miller (Eds.), *Handbook of psychology: Educational psychology* (Vol. 7, pp. 511-530). New York: Wiley.

Wampold, B. E. (2001). *The great psychotherapy debate: Models, methods and findings*. Mahwah, NJ: Erlbaum.

Watkins, A., & Kurtz, P. D. (2001). Using solution-focused intervention to address African-American male overrepresentation in special education: A case study. *Children & Schools, 23*(4), 223-235.

Webster-Stratton, C., & Taylor, T. (2001). Nipping early risk factors in the bud. *Prevention Science, 2*(3), 165-192.

Weissberg, R., & Durlak, J. (2007). SEL Meta-analysis. Retrieved August 15, 2007, from http://www.casel.org/sel/meta.php

Wolchik, S. A., Sandler, I. N., Millsap, R. E., Plummer, B. A., Greene, S. M., Anderson, E. R., et al. (2002). Six-year follow-up of preventive interventions for children of divorce: A randomized controlled trial. *JAMA, 288*, 1874-1881.

Wolraich, M. L., Wibbelsman, C. J., & Brown, T. (2005). ADHD among adolescents. *Pediatrics, 115*(6), 1734-1745.

Woolley, M. E., & Bowen, G. L. (2007). In the context of risk: Supportive adults and the school engagement of middle school students. *Family Relations, 56*, 92-104.

Ysseldyke, J. (2001). Reflections on a research career. *Exceptional Children, 67*(3), 295-309.

Zentall, S. S. (2005). Theory and evidence-based strategies for children with attentional problems. *Psychology in the schools, 42*(8), 821-836.

Index

Note: Page numbers in *italics* refer to figures, tables and boxes.